The Dictionary of
Computer Graphics
and Virtual Reality

Second Edition

Roy Latham

The Dictionary of Computer Graphics and Virtual Reality

Second Edition

With 18 Diagrams

Springer-Verlag

New York Berlin Heidelberg London Paris
Tokyo Hong Kong Barcelona Budapest

Roy Latham
Computer Graphics Systems
  Development Corporation
Mountain View, CA 94043-2350
USA

The first edition of this work, published in 1991, was entitled *The Dictionary of Computer Graphics Technology and Applications*.

Library of Congress Cataloging-in-Publication Data
Roy Latham.
       The dictionary of computer graphics and virtual reality /
    Roy Latham. — 2nd ed.
           p.   cm.
       Includes bibliographical references.
       ISBN 0-387-94405-2
       1. Computer graphics—Dictionaries. 2. Virtual reality—
    Dictionaries. I. Title.
    T385.L38   1995
    006.6'03—dc20   94-36569

Printed on acid-free paper.

Production managed by Laura Carlson; manufacturing supervised by Genieve Shaw.
Photocomposed copy prepared from the author's file.
Printed and bound by R.R. Donnelley and Sons, Harrisonburg, VA.
Printed in the United States of America.

9 8 7 6 5 4 3 2 1

ISBN 0-387-94405-2 Springer-Verlag New York Berlin Heidelberg

Contents

Using This Dictionary

What's Included

This dictionary is a revised expansion of the author's earlier *Dictionary of Computer Graphics Technology and Applications*. The main addition is the new terminology related to virtual reality, as rich a source of new jargon as any around. New terminology has been added for robotics and telepresence, especially insofar as they are allied with virtual reality. More terminology has been added in the field of networked simulation, another growth area.

Some terminology from the previous work related to companies and products—hot items just a few years ago but now passé—has been dropped. Some publishing terminology has been swept out on the grounds that it now belongs to its own specialists.

This dictionary is designed for both relative novices and professionals working with computer graphics and virtual reality. Those new to the field are struck by the maze of jargon posing an obstacle to understanding. Those who know their specialty well are confronted by new frontiers of terminology in dealing with applications areas or with specialists in different areas. A person who is an expert in, say, desktop publishing, will rarely need this dictionary to translate the jargon of that area, but may find it useful in unraveling the claims of competing graphics hardware.

Terminology is included from allied technologies including image processing, electronics, general computing, video, hardware engineering, software engineering, workstations, color science, and project management. Terms from allied technologies are included to serve developers of products, who may be served by definitions even if the terms are not strictly a part of computer graphics or virtual reality applications. Also included are key terms from the most widespread application areas of computer graphics, including desktop publishing, animation, scientific visualization, electrical and mechanical computer-aided design, and business graphics.

One of the challenges of putting together this dictionary has been deciding what to include and what to exclude. Ultimately, the test has been to include terms that are most likely to be faced by computer graphics developers and users, and those that are most likely to be unfamiliar or cause confusion.

The most difficult cases for inclusion and exclusion are companies and products. Leaving these out altogether would omit a great deal of importance, since many people need knowledge about the workings of the industry. But including certain companies and products leads to leaving out others, and there is always a risk of unknowingly excluding something or someone important in a particular specialty. Also, the fortunes of products and companies can change overnight. Consequently, relatively few companies and products are included, but I hope enough are included to give a sense of the industry and the products that are offered.

An objective of this dictionary is to provide definitions comprising only other entries in the dictionary, in the senses defined, plus standard English. Consequently, insofar as this objective has been achieved, reference to a standard dictionary should resolve the meanings of terms not defined here.

Abbreviations

Most of the alphabet soup that people, myself included, call acronyms are really abbreviations, an acronym being the crowning achievement of an abbreviation reaching the status of a full-blown word, like *radar*, spelled out in lower case. In this dictionary, abbreviations are decoded into the word sequence from which they were derived and then defined under the same entry. Attaching the definition to the abbreviation rather than the word sequence is done on the grounds that it was probably the acronym that was encountered by the reader rather than the spelled-out version. The few exceptions are when an acronym is used less frequently than its full version.

Abbreviations are alphabetized as if they were words, rather than being entered at the start of the listings for each letter. Words beginning with numbers are alphabetized as if the number was spelled out, for example "3-D" is alphabetized as if it were "three-D." However, numbers not at the beginning of a word are alphabetized as if the digits "0 ... 9" preceded "a"; this, for example, yields P0, P1, and P2 as sequential entries. Terms having two or more words are alphabetized ignoring the blanks separating the words.

Pronunciation and Parts of Speech

Pronunciation is provided in backslashes after the word for entries where standard English does not apply, for example WYSIWYG *wizzy-wig*\. Letters to be pronounced individually by name, as often occurs in abbreviations, are capitalized and separated by dashes. For example, EEPROM has the first two Es pronounced as the name of the letter E and PROM pronounced as a word, \E-E-prom\. Other pronunciations are given by approximating the sounds with English words or fragments whose pronunciations are less ambiguous.

The part of speech is provided, abbreviated and in italics. (The abbreviations are noun *n.*, transitive verb *v.t.*, intransitive verb *v.i.*, adjective *adj.*, and preposition *prep.*) Notes about the origin, technical discipline, or alternate spelling are sometimes included in square brackets after the word or pronunciation.

File Name Extensions

File name extensions are codes of typically three letters added to the right-hand side of a period when naming a file on a computer. Certain extensions have achieved a degree of standardization in signifying how the data contained in the file should be interpreted. In fact, sometimes the extension ends up as the only clue as to how the file should be interpreted.

Accordingly, a number of these common extensions are included for reference. To help distinguish these bits of computer esoterica from ordinary words or abbreviations, a sans-serif typeface is used for entries that correspond to file name extensions, for example: PIC.

Alternates and Cross-References

There are variations in fine points of spelling for a number of common computer graphics terms, for example, *scan line vs. scanline vs. scan-line.* In such cases, I have attempted to accumulate one or two dozen citations by different authors in scholarly works and to use the most common as the main entry. Alternates are listed if they appear at least twice and in more than 10 percent of the total number of occurrences. A similar but somewhat stricter rule is used for alternate meanings.

Technical people are fond of creating product names that have unexpected capital letters in the middle of a word, combine capital letters and small capitals, or make interesting use of subscripts and superscripts. I have tried to preserve these as intended by their originators, but except for the mixtures of upper and lower case, which are easy to reproduce, few people other than the originators attempt such care.

Cross-references are provided to synonymous and related terms. The cross-referenced terms are given in all capitals. Synonymous terms or definitions appear after a colon. Related terms that bear directly on the definition of the term follow the key construct "—See," or if less directly related "—See also." Terms for opposites or for competing methods follow "—Compare."

References and Word List

Appended to this dictionary is a bibliography providing a good set of basic reference texts for those wishing fuller expositions of many of the terms and concepts introduced in this dictionary. These texts provide hundreds of additional references to the subject-matter literature. Also appended is an expanded word list designed to facilitate the spell-checking of words often omitted from spelling lists for general use.

Corrections and Additions

Computer graphics is just now approaching middle age as a discipline. Not all of the terminology has settled into standard usage. This dictionary attempts to conform to the most widely adopted usage and to suggest known alternatives. Readers, however, must be alert to local variations in usage.

The attributions made for the origins of terms are based on the earliest reference found, or upon a similar attribution made by someone else. In only a few cases have the cited originators explicitly noted coining the terminology, so it is, in many cases, possible that the terminology predated the particular appearance in print. The author would be grateful to readers who can contribute knowledge of the origins or history of the terminology, or who otherwise note corrections or additions to this dictionary.

The author may be reached via the Internet electronic-mail network with the address roy_w_latham@cup.portal.com, or by writing in care of the publisher.

Acknowledgments

I gratefully acknowledge the valuable contributions of my wife, P.Y. Cheng, for reviewing the technical content of the present volume and the previous work on which it is based. Lawrence Adams purged the present manuscript of many typographical and stylistic errors, which contributed substantially to the work.

The author remains grateful to those who helped in preparation of the first edition, *The Dictionary of Computer Graphics Technology and Applications*, from which the present work evolved. Sun Microsystems, Inc., provided support in the preparation of much of the early manuscript for that book. I am also grateful to Bob Ellis, David Rosenthal, and Mike Shantz, my former colleagues at Sun, who made suggestions concerning the manuscript. Special thanks to Sun colleagues Susan Carrie, Jack McKeown, Jayna Pike, Stuart Wells, and Johnson Yan, each of whom thoroughly reviewed the manuscript and made many valuable comments. I am indebted to Mark Hall and John Barry at Sun for their encouragement and promotion of the earlier work.

Then and now, thanks go to William Gladstone and Matt Wagner at Waterside Productions, and to the editors and reviewers at Springer-Verlag, who contributed significantly to getting this dictionary into your hands.

A

ABI : *Applications Binary Interface*; the low-level interface conventions for a graphics or software system, specified for use by applications programmers and other system users.

abscissa *n.* : The x component of an (x,y) coordinate pair. The y component is the *ordinate*.

absolute *adj.* : Defined with respect to a fixed origin. In graphics, with respect to a fixed coordinate system rather than relative to the last point plotted or drawn to.

A-buffering *n.* : A modification to z-buffering to facilitate antialiasing in which a pointer may be stored instead of the z-value, so that a stack of data for partially covering faces may be built for pixels having such contributions, with the pixel stacks being resolved as the last step in rendering.

accelerator *n.* : A graphics accelerator; specialized hardware dedicated to increasing the speed with which graphics operations are performed. Usually, the graphics accelerator is assumed to contain the frame buffer and video output electronics, but sometimes the frame buffer is considered a separate entity driven by the accelerator. Also, **accelerate** *v.t.* : to speed up by processing through an accelerator.

accelerator port : In a graphics accelerator, the hardware interface, which receives data for processing through the accelerator, as opposed to the *direct (frame buffer) port*, which allows access to individual pixels without going through the accelerator.

acceptance test procedure : A formal means for determining if a system meets its specified performance characteristics, usually as a condition for customer payment.

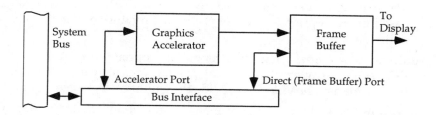

1

accommodation *n.* : The ability of the eye to focus over a range of distances; the range over which the eye focuses.

achromatic *adj.* 1 : Without color, such as black, gray, or white. 2 : Of a lens, able to focus at least two colors in a common plane.

acknowledgment *n.* : An output to an operator from a graphics application indicating that a trigger event, such as the click of a mouse button, has been received and is being processed.

ACM *A-C-M*\ : *Association for Computing Machinery*; society for computer professionals; the parent organization of *SIGGRAPH*.

acoustic environment *n.* : the set of sounds and sound-generating locations that characterize a space, especially as they are modeled for a virtual environment.

acoustic tablet : SONIC TABLET.

active database [mainly flight simulator terminology] : A subset of on-line graphics data stored so as to be accessible for interactive use with a graphics system. Typically, the whole database is stored on disk, with the active database selected from it and kept in random access memory. : **active storage.**

activity network : A chart used for project planning in which tasks are summarized in boxes and interconnected by lines that imply the order in which tasks must be done. It differs from a PERT chart in that tasks, not milestones, are in the boxes.

adaptation : The ability of the eye to adjust its sensitivity to light by varying the size of the pupil and, principally, by chemically varying the sensitivity of the retina.

adaptive forward differencing : —See AFD.

adaptive sampling : Adjusting the sampling density for a graphics calculation in response to characteristics of the object being rendered; for example, performing higher-density occlusion sampling near an object's edges.

adaptive subdivision : Adjusting the sizes of polygons in a mesh approximating a curved surface, where the size of each polygon is based upon its projected size or the local curvature of the surface, or both.

additive color model : The color model appropriate to mixing colored light sources (rather than inks or paints), in which red, green, and blue primaries are added to provide the gamut of displayed colors.

addressability *n.* 1 : In a digital memory, the ability to access data in small segments; for example, a system offering a minimum of **byte addressability** implies that each byte in the memory may be individually accessed and retrieved, but that an individual bit can only be accessed as part of a byte. 2 : In a graphics system, the precision with which the screen coordinates may be specified. **Subpixel addressability** usually implies that either antialiasing mechanisms spread the graphics to two or more pixels, or that different round-off to whole pixels will occur during the drawing.

AFD : *Adaptive Forward Differencing;* a method for rendering images of curved surfaces that adjusts the rendering within the image to take into account the correct amount of detail needed for the particular surface, viewpoint, and display resolution.

affine map : Any transformation composed only of translations, rotations, scalings, and shears.

aiming symbol : A circle or other symbol functioning as a tracking cross for a light pen.

AIX \ *A-I-X* \ : IBM Corp. operating system, a version of UNIX.

algebraic surface : A surface defined as the locus points where a given algebraic function is equal to a constant, usually zero.

algorithm *n.* : An unambiguous sequence of steps for performing a logical or mathematical process. An algorithm is distinct from its implementation, typically as a computer program or in specialized hardware.

alias *n.* 1 : A list of electronic-mail addresses serving as the distribution list for a particular topic. 2 : Any name that substitutes for another name, especially in the context of UNIX or UNIX commands.

aliasing *n.* : The visible artifacts that result from producing an image by sampling an underlying conceptual image having higher spatial frequencies than the sample frequency; includes moiré patterns in fine detail, breakup of thin lines into dots, and stairstepping of surface edges. Note that subpixel occlusion errors and quantization errors may produce similar artifacts, but are error sources distinct from aliasing.

alpha channel : Memory associated with each pixel used to store, as either a value or an occlusion mask, the fractional coverage of the pixel. The data may be output along with the color video signals to facilitate compositing of video images.

alpha-geometric *adj.* : Related to being drawn with graphics primitives, rather than formed with character symbols.

alpha-mosaic *adj.* : Related to being formed with character symbols, rather than drawn with graphics primitives.

alphanumeric *n.* 1 : A character that is neither a control character nor part of a control sequence. Includes letters, numbers, and punctuation. 2 [uncommon] : A character that is either a letter or a number. Also, *adj.*: being in the set of alphanumerics.

alpha test : The initial test of a new product after the design team has fixed the obvious problems, but before there is enough confidence to sell it to customers. An **internal alpha test** exposes the product to new users within the organization, and an **external alpha test** to selected users outside the organization.

ambient light : In a graphics lighting model, the constant nondirectional illumination generally applied to each object in a scene to approximate the effect of light from scattered reflection. Outdoors, the ambient light from the hemisphere of the blue sky is about 20 percent of the direct illumination from the sun.

anaglyph *n.* : a stereo image in which views for the left and right eyes are presented in different colors, typically red and blue, for viewing through corresponding filters for each eye.

AND *and*\ [usually all caps, even though it is not an abbreviation, to distinguish its use as a logic function from the standard use as a conjunction] *n.* 1: A logic function in which the output is true if and only if both inputs are true. 2: The result of applying the AND function <C is the AND of signals A and B>. Also, *v.t.* : To perform the AND function. Also, ANDs, ANDed, ANDing.

animation *n.* 1 : The application of computer graphics for the preparation of moving sequences for commercial advertising, education, or other purposes; often in video format and usually having the sequence as the end product. 2 : Any graphic method where the illusion of motion is produced by rapid viewing of individually generated frames in a sequence.

anisotropic transformation : A mapping that does not preserve the ratio of heights to widths; by which, for example, squares would be transformed to rectangles.

annotation text : Text that is not subject to a transformation pipeline, but rather is always displayed in a predetermined size and orientation; —Compare structure text.

ANSI *ansy*\ *n.* : American National Standards Institute; organization providing standards for computer graphics interfaces such as GKS, among other things. Also, *adj.* : ANSI-originated <an ANSI standard>.

antialiasing [*alt.* anti-aliasing; the unhyphenated form is slightly preferred] *n.* : Filtering an underlying image to eliminate spatial frequencies greater than that corresponding to the rate sampled for pixels, thereby eliminating the artifacts of aliasing such as line break-up and edge staircasing. In practice, antialiasing treatments are often applied as the individual primitives are rendered, rather than to the whole image, sometimes at the expense of introducing other artifacts. Note that antialiasing methods are generally applied before sampling for rendering, so artifacts are properly said to be *prevented,* and not to be *removed.* The uncommon exceptions are techniques that attempt to deduce the underlying input from rendered output, for example, by recognizing a stairstepped boundary as an edge. Also, **antialias** *v.t.* : to apply antialiasing.

aperture *n.* : The usually circular, light-admitting area of a camera lens (typically having its diameter determined by an adjustable diaphragm), or the corresponding element in a computer graphics model. In computer graphics the aperture is modeled for depth of focus and highlight effects.

API : *Application Programmer's Interface;* the style and usage conventions that determine the "look and feel" of a graphics user interface as they appear to an end user.

Apollo Computers, Inc. : One of the companies pioneering engineering workstations; now part of Hewlett-Packard, Inc.

apostilb *n.* : An international unit of luminance equal to 0.1 milli-lambert.

application program : The end-user software employing graphics and computer products; as distinct from system users, like a window system or graphics library, which also use the products.

application programmer's interface : —See API.

applications binary interface : —See ABI.

application specific integrated circuit : —See ASIC.

Application Visualization System : —See AVS.

APT *apt*\\ : *Automatically Programmed Tool;* a venerable programming language for describing the motion of tools in numerically controlled machining equipment.

arbitration *n.* : For a computer bus, a protocol for determining which of competing modules requesting the bus shall be given control.

arc *n.* 1 : A portion of a circle, sometimes generalized to include portions of an ellipse. 2 : In the design of typefaces, a curved stroke part of a character that does not enclose an area.

architect *v.t.* : To design the architecture of.

architecture *n.* 1 : The design of a system at the level of functional modules and interconnections, generally with sufficient details so that individual functions may be successfully designed and implemented without full knowledge of systems requirements. 2 : In the context of computer systems or networks, the type of connected computer or workstation as categorized by the processor chip used in the machine; e.g., a SPARC architecture or a 386 architecture.

archiving *n.* : Saving digital data for future reference, especially in the context of special hardware or software designed to support storage and retrieval. Also, **archive** *v.t.* : to perform archiving.

area block : In flight simulation graphics, one of a number of usually equal-sized square or triangular regions comprising a database of terrain and terrain features. Area blocks are typically used to facilitate data retrieval and sometimes prioritization.

area sampling : An antialiasing technique for computing the displayed color and intensity of a pixel based upon area-weighted contributions of the graphics objects to the pixel area; —Compare point sampling.

ARPA : *A*dvanced *R*esearch *P*roject *A*gency; an agency of the U.S. government sponsoring many, typically high-risk, research projects. The agency was named DARPA for awhile, the *D* for *Defense*.

ARPANET : *A*dvanced *R*esearch *P*roject *A*gency *NET*work; pioneering computer network, developed by a U.S. Department of Defense agency, linking industry, schools, and government.

articulated object : A graphics database construction having parts that move relative to one another, such as is used to represent a robotic arm or aircraft wing flaps.

artifact *n.* : A visible error in a displayed image, usually due to a simplification or cost-saving measure rather than an implementation error. Aliasing, quantization errors, and subpixel-occlusion errors are different sources of artifacts in graphics images.

artificial object [mainly flight simulation terminology] : A graphics object used for culling or other purposes, which is ultimately not displayed in the rendered image.

artificial reality [coined by Myron Kreuger, before other terms came in vogue, as the title of his book published in 1982] : VIRTUAL REALITY : virtual environment.

ascent line : In typography, a horizontal line corresponding to the maximum height of any character in the character set.

ASCII *ask-ee*\\ : *A*merican *S*tandard *C*ode for *I*nformation *I*nterchange; a standard encoding of text and control characters into binary.

ASIC *A-sick*\ : *A*pplication *S*pecific *I*ntegrated *C*ircuit; a gate-array, standard cell, or other nonstandard integrated circuit chip designed for proprietary use. Note that it is not the technology with which the circuit was fabricated that makes it an ASIC, but rather its restriction to proprietary use.

aspect *n.* : A nongeometric property of a graphics primitive, such as its color.

aspect ratio 1 : The ratio of width to height, particularly for a rectangular region such as a pixel or the rectangle enclosing a character. 2 : The ratio of width to height of a display. For example, the standard television monitor aspect ratio is 4 : 3. 3 : The ratio of width to height of a character or symbol.

assert *v.t.* : In an electronic circuit, to put a control signal in the state where control action is initiated.

Association for Computing Machinery : —See ACM.

AT *A-T*\ : *A*dvanced *T*echnology; originally, an IBM PC/AT personal computer having an Intel 80286 processor and a 16-bit I/O bus. Now used generally for IBM-compatible 80286-based personal computers.

ATG : *A*utomatic *T*est *G*enerator; option in the Genesis design package used to produce test vectors for fault coverage; or, more generally, for similar packages in other electronic design systems.

atmosphere *n.* : In computer graphics, the class of visual effects associated with modeling the earth's atmosphere, especially haze, fog, or light attenuation. —See also, FADING.

atom *n.* : The smallest piece of work that cannot be interrupted on a processor. For example, most computer central processing units do not allow simple instructions like LOAD or ADD to be interrupted. They are atoms and must be completed before handling an external interrupt. For graphics hardware, there is often a broad design issue of which operations to make atomic.

atomic *adj.* 1 : Related to a type of processor state that can be updated in only one (uninterruptible) instruction. 2 : Having all of the necessary elements present within a compact format, as might be desired in a low-level graphics interface.

attenuation *n.* : The decrease of light energy due to absorption by its medium of propagation, such as by travel through the atmosphere.

attribute *n.* 1 : A property associated with a graphics primitive, generally affecting a rendering characteristic other than its underlying geometry, such as color, line width, or pattern. 2: In PHIGS, any of several properties and processing variables associated with an output primitive, including the transformation and viewing matrices to be used while processing the primitive.

auditory feedback *n.* : sound, especially as the term occurs in scientific papers.

autoconfiguration *n.* : A process by which software in a host processor on a computer system may determine the configuration of the system, including automatic identification of the modules connected to buses.

autocorrelation *n.* : In signal and image processing, the correlation of a process with itself as a function of space or time. For example, if in a video sequence the autocorrelation of pixel intensity at a particular address as a function of time was equal to one for all time increments, that would imply the pixel intensity never changed from frame to frame; an autocorrelation of zero would imply the pixel intensity changed unpredictably from frame to frame.

autodimensioning *n.* : In a drafting program, a program feature that computes and annotates the size of drawn elements.

Autofact : Conference traditionally held in the United States (Detroit or Chicago) in early November, dealing with design tools, many graphics oriented, applied to the automobile industry. Sponsored by the Society of Manufacturing Engineers.

automatic brightness control : A means for automatically controlling the brightness of a display in response to changes in ambient light.

A/UX : A variant of the UNIX™ operating system for Apple Macintosh computers.

AVS : *Application Visualization System*; high-level graphics software interface originated by Stellar Computer, Inc.

B

back clipping plane : a plane perpendicular to the line of sight for clipping out distant objects. : the YON plane.

backfacing *adj.* : In a graphics database being rendered, with respect to a polygon having an associated normal vector, having the polygon normal vector pointed away from the current eyepoint. If a backfacing polygon is part of a convex polyhedron of opaque polygons viewed from outside the polyhedron, then the backfacing polygon will always be occluded from view and may be eliminated from further processing as soon as it is found to be backfacing. In other cases, the graphics system must establish conventions with respect to color and illumination for rendering the backfacing sides of polygons.

background *n.* 1 : A predetermined image processed as the lowest priority (for two-dimensional) or most distant (for three-dimensional) graphics object, thereby providing a default image for regions in which no other graphics primitive is rendered. 2 : In electrostatic printing technology, unwanted toner particles in print areas intended to be unmarked. Also, *adj.* : related to the default background.

background color 1 : The default color to which every pixel in a window is to be initialized. 2 : The color to be used for the zeros when a binary pattern is to be translated into two colors for graphics display. 3 : The set of pixels in a window that remain untouched after a series of graphics operations; all that remains after pixels of interest have been written.

backing store : In a windows system, stored portions of the raster screen saved when they are occluded, so that they may be written back to the screen when later exposed.

backplane *n.* : An assembly having circuit board connectors and interconnecting wiring, and usually not active circuit components, for distributing power and providing communication among sub-assemblies in an electronic system.

back porch [from the appearance of the waveform on an oscilloscope] : In the composite video signal for television, the portion of the blanking pulse that contains the burst signal used for synchronizing the color oscillator.

backwards ray-tracing : Ray-tracing in which the computations are performed as if the rays traveled from the viewpoint to the light sources, hence, backwards with respect to the physical propagation. Currently the standard means for ordering ray-tracing computations.

bandwidth *n.* : The ability of a bus, interface, or device to transfer digital information, usually expressed in millions of bytes per second. More carefully designated **bus bandwidth.**

bang [UNIX *slang*] : The exclamation point, "!"

bar chart : A graph in which data values are represented by rectangular regions having lengths proportionate to the values.

Bar Charts

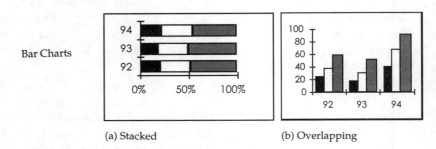

(a) Stacked   (b) Overlapping

barfogenic zone [*slang,* also *barfonic region*] *n.* : Nauseating to the point of inducing vomiting, as of a virtual reality system inducing motion sickness.

barrel distortion [the sides of a rectangle bow to look like the outline of a barrel] : A display system defect causing images to bulge outwards toward the edges of the screen.

basis spline : B-spline.

basis weight : The weight of a specified area of paper; for example, the weight in pounds of 3,000 square feet of paper, the area corresponding to a ream (500 sheets) of 24-inch x 36-inch sheets.

baud rate *bawd rate*\ [from J.E. Baudot, inventor of a serial code for telegraphy] : rate of serial transmission in bits per second. Now used with RS-232 transmission protocols in which there is a start bit, seven or eight data bits, an optional parity bit, and one or two stop bits. In all, there are about 10 bits transmitted per character of data, so, for example, 9600 baud corresponds to 960 bytes per second.

beam-penetration display : Type of color CRT display having layers of red and green phosphors applied to the faceplate, wherein the voltage applied to accelerate the electron beam varies the depth of penetration and thus the color. Has advantages of simplicity and higher resolution than shadow mask designs, but the device can only produce shades of red, orange, yellow, and green—not blue. Hence it is now largely supplanted by shadow mask technology. The beam-penetration tube itself is also called a *penetron*.

beam position : In a graphics system having a calligraphic display, the current position of the spot on the screen from which subsequent relative drawing commands will originate.

beam tracing : A variation of *ray-tracing* using a polygonal cone for the intersection computations rather than a single line (ray). The objective is to take advantage of the coherence of adjacent rays to minimize computations.

bed of nails 1 : OCCLUSION MASK. 2 : Fixture having many pinlike probes, used to test printed circuit boards.

beige *n.* : A popular office color, synonyms for which include: almond, camel, gravel, atmosphere, elmwood, meerchaum, belleek, folkstone, smog, biarritz, ecru, vinoso-bubalinus, biscuit, fumosus, champagne, griseo-sepiaceus, bronze clair, cuban sand, doe, grain, cobweb, mauve blush, mavis, miami sand, nougat, nude, pawnee, pecan, seasand, avellaneous, drab, and bisque. The U.S. National Institute of Standards and Technology (formerly, National Bureau of Standards) *Dictionary of Color Names* is full of such information.

benchmark *n.* : A program, application package, or defined set of algorithms and data ported to various computer systems for the purpose of comparing processing speeds. Some benchmarks attempt to isolate very specific areas of performance, and others to provide a mix of computational work characteristic of a particular type of system use. General graphics benchmarks include the number of 10 pixel-length randomly oriented vectors or 100 pixel-area randomly oriented triangles a system can render in one second. Also, *v.t.* : to collect performance data by running a benchmark; *adj.* : having the characteristics of a benchmark.

Beta™ [Sony] *n.* : A format for recording television video on half-inch-tape cassettes.

Beta spline [originated by Brian Barsky] : A type of curve used for graphics modeling, derived as a generalization of uniform cubic B-splines and providing parameters for local control of bias and tension of the curves.

beta test : Shipments of a new product to customers who agree to use the product prior to general distribution and to report problems encountered in their applications. —Compare ALPHA TEST.

bezel *n.* : A frame surrounding the face of a CRT in a display system.

Bezier curve *bez-ee-ay*\ : A type of curve defined as a function-weighted sum of control points. A Bezier curve always lies within the convex hull of its control points. The curves have properties that make them useful in computer-aided mechanical design. **Bezier surfaces** are straightforward extensions of the curves.

BiCMOS *by-see-mos*\ *adj.* : Having bipolar and CMOS devices fabricated in the same integrated circuit. Bipolar devices provide higher drive capabilities and I/O compatibility, while CMOS has advantages of low power and high circuit density. Also, *n.* : A BiCMOS semiconductor process or product family.

bilinear interpolation : Interpolation among three or four points arranged as vertices of a triangle or quadrilateral by linearly interpolating to a common coordinate value (typically the y value) on each of two edges, and then again in the other coordinate value (typically x).

bill of materials : —See BOM.

binary space partition tree [*alt.* binary separating plane tree] : A means of subdividing three-dimensional space by using planes, possibly arbitrarily oriented, which successively halve the space at each partition. The partitioning corresponds to a tree structure of partitioned spaces and planes and is useful in determining priorities for hidden surface removal.

binding *n.* 1 : The association of more generally defined parameters and functions with the subprogram names and formal parameters of a specific computer language; such as the C-language *binding* of a graphics interface. 2 : The process by which a computer on a network finds a server to provide it with certain services.

binocular *adj.* : Using the stereo capability of vision with two eyes, such as related to a display apparatus making use of different images for each eye to provide a stereo image.

binocular disparity : The difference in perspective of the views from the two *eyes* of an observer resulting from the separate positions of the eyes.

biocular *adj.* : Using two eyes, often as related to a display apparatus that presents an image for each eye even though the two images may be identical. –Compare BINOCULAR.

BIT \bit\ *n.* : *Built-In Test*; the mechanisms included within an electronic system to perform functional tests without external equipment. Also, *adj.* : of or related to BIT. Sometimes used redundantly <system BIT test>.

bit [*bi*nary dig*it*] *n.* : A one or zero in a binary number; the smallest unit of information stored in a digital memory.

bitblt \bitblit\ [*alt.* bit-blt] *n.* : *Bit Bl*ock *T*ransfer; movement or copying of a bit-mapped image to a new location through the use of simple logical operations at the source or destination, or both. The objective is to transfer the image at high speed by avoiding the use of intermediate storage. Also, *v.t.* : to move data using a bitblt : to blit.

bit map [*alt.* bitmap] : A two-dimensional pattern of ones and zeros intended for ultimate use in a graphics image; commonly used to represent text characters and the like. Also, **bit-map** *v.t.* : to represent using a bit map.

bit-plane [*alt.* bit plane] : One bit of memory defined over a two-dimensional address space, especially such memory comprising part of a frame buffer. The concept may derive from visualizing the pixel memory arrayed in the z dimension of an (x,y) addressed frame buffer, so that the corresponding bits of each word of memory lie in a plane. A frame buffer might, for example, be said to have two cursor planes, meaning two bits of the memory associated with each pixel in the frame buffer is dedicated to storing data for the cursor.

bit-plane encoding : In image processing, image compression by application of run-length encoding to each bit-plane of the pixels of an image.

bit-sliced processor : A computer processor built of circuit elements that are designed to be linked in increments of typically four or eight bits so as to provide processing of longer word lengths. Bit-sliced processors have traditionally been used in the design of custom high-performance equipment for graphics and image processing. The designs usually feature a wide (typically 100 bits or more) instruction word and multiple arithmetic units. In some applications, the bit-sliced design approach has been superseded by the use of standard DSP chips.

blackbody *n.* : An idealized object producing a reproducible spectrum of light as a function of temperature used as a means for specifying the color of illuminants in the yellow-white to blue-white region depending upon temperature. Also, *adj.* : related to a blackbody <blackbody radiation>.

blacker-than-black : —See BLANKING LEVEL.

black level *n.* : In a video signal, the voltage level corresponding to a completely black video input in the displayable (nonblanked) portion of the video.

blanking *n.* : In a CRT display, the process of shutting off the electron beam while the deflection circuits are repositioned to start the display of a new line or frame. Also, **blank** *v.t.* : to apply blanking.

blanking level : In a video signal, the voltage level during blanking designed to ensure that the electron beam is completely suppressed. : PEDESTAL LEVEL : BLACKER-THAN-BLACK level.

bleed *n.* : In the layout of a published page, a photograph that extends through the margin all the way to the top or side edge.

bleeding *n.* 1 : The appearance of colored light on a surface due to diffuse reflection from another surface : BOUNCE LIGHT. 2 : CRT display anomaly in which the color of one pixel affects neighboring pixels. Also, *adj.* : exhibiting bleeding.

bleeding white : A display system defect in which white areas appear to flow into black areas.

blending *n.* : LEVEL-OF-DETAIL BLENDING.

blendmap [VEX terminology] *n.* : An indexed table whose output controls the proportions of mixing input video pixels with graphics pixels on a pixel-by-pixel basis.

blend surface : In a graphics model, a surface added to provide a continuous transition between two other intersecting surfaces. : FILLET : JOIN SURFACE.

blinking *n.* : A means of highlighting a graphics object or text by changing the color or intensity between two values periodically, usually a few times per second. The frequency of change is the **blink rate.** Also, **blink** *v.t.* : to apply blinking.

blob [Originated by James Blinn] *n.* : A generalization of an algebraic surface, defined as the locus of points of constant value of superimposed exponential density functions. The surface yields a quadratic equation suited to ray tracing, producing forms appearing as ellipsoids that smoothly blend together.

block-normalized *adj.* : Having a format for binary numbers in which the implied binary point is moved among groups of (typically four) bits. The approach is used mainly in dedicated hardware to provide a range of numbers greater than fixed point representation, but without the implementation complexity of a floating point representation.

blondel : A unit of luminance equal to 0.1 millilambert.

blooming : A usually undesired condition of a video camera or display system, due to excessive brightness, in which a white portion of the image grows to encompass regions that would otherwise be darker.

bodysuit *n.* : A form-fitting garment having position and angle sensors by which the relative positions of the parts of the wearer's body are measured and communicated to a computer. The measurements permit the construction of a graphics image that mimics the posture of the wearer in a scene.

BOM *bomb*\\ : *Bill Of M*aterials; the official list of parts, including the part numbers, used by purchasing and manufacturing departments in an organization to buy parts for building a product.

booting *n.* : The start-up process for a computer system, including application of power, determination of system configuration, and initial installation of the operating system. With respect to graphics systems, the process may include identification of the frame buffer parameters, loading of the initial display font, and, if more than one type of monitor is supported, determination of the monitor parameters and subsequent setup of the video format. Also, **boot** *v.t.*: to initiate booting.

boot-time *n.* : During system booting.

bottleneck *n.* 1 : The processing stage or other critical factor that limits an aspect of system performance. For example, the bottleneck in a graphics system's ability to render triangles might be either the ability to transform vertices or the ability to write pixels. 2 : A problem in warping an image in two passes, in which the first pass collapses many pixels to one, and the second pass expands one to many.

bounce light : BLEEDING.

boundary representation : Modeling of a solid object by specification of the surfaces of the object, as opposed to representation by intersection of solids (using CSG).

bounding box : A rectangular polyhedron constructed around a graphics object, usually with edges parallel to the coordinate axes, for simplified clip testing, culling, or intersection testing.

bounding volume : Any mathematically simpler surface enclosing a graphics object for the purposes of culling or intersection tests. —Compare ARTIFICIAL OBJECT, BOUNDING BOX, BUBBLE TEST, CONVEX HULL.

box filter : A convolution kernel having uniform amplitude over the region corresponding to a pixel, and zero elsewhere.

breezeway [from the appearance of the waveform on an oscilloscope; a breezeway is a passage connecting a house to a garage] *n.* : The portion of a composite video waveform in the back porch between the synchronization pulse and the color burst.

B-rep [*alt.* b-rep] : —See BOUNDARY REPRESENTATION.

Bresenham's algorithm : A widely used algorithm for rasterizing lines by generating successive unit increments in either the horizontal or vertical direction. A variation of the algorithm rasterizes circles.

brightness *n.* 1 : The perceived amount of light, depending upon the luminance and chrominance of the source. Since the eye does not perceive all frequencies of radiant energy equally, a light source may contain more physical energy but not be as bright as a second source that corresponds better to the eye's sensitivity. 2 : Mainly in the context of publishing, the amount of lighter shades in an image relative to the amount of darker shades. In this context, a preponderance of lighter shades corresponds to a brighter image.

brilliant *adj.* : Having both high color value and high color saturation : being comparatively light and pure in color.

B-spline : Basis spline; a type of spline curve, closely related to Bezier curves, but with additional properties of local control and continuity that are useful for curve fitting and modeling.

BSP tree : —See BINARY SPACE PARTITION TREE.

bubble test : A form of clip test in which an off-line-computed sphere surrounding a portion of a three-dimensional graphics database is compared with the clip region.

buffer *n.* : An area of temporary storage used, for example, to hold data awaiting further processing or transfer to a hardware device. Also, *v.t.* : to store in a buffer. —See also, FRAME BUFFER, DOUBLE-BUFFER.

buffer raster : A graphics data object that designates a rectangular region of nonscreen preferred memory.

bug *n.* : A defect in computer software or, more generally, in any part of a computer hardware or software system. The term originated in the days of computers using electromechanical relays, when an insect was found to be causing a fault in a contact closure. Now more often used to refer to a design defect rather than a component failure.

bug list : A list of known discrepancies between a product's specifications and its current implementation, often including suggestions for temporary workarounds.

build *n.* : A software package compiled and linked directly and entirely from source code, usually for a formal release so that the correspondence to known source code is established.

bump mapping [originated by James Blinn] : A texture mapping applied by perturbing the directions of the surface normals of a graphics object so that shading provides the appearance of a nonsmooth surface with respect to illumination, while the surface remains geometrically smooth.

bundle table : In the GKS and PHIGS graphics standards, a table of workstation-dependent aspects for a particular primitive.

burst *n.* : COLOR BURST.

bus *n.* : A means of electronically communicating data among two or more units within a system, typically involving a binary number of data signals (commonly 16 or 32, for example), plus additional control signals. Often similar communications means outside of a single electronic enclosure is designated a *network* rather than a bus, but there are many exceptions.

bus bandwidth : —See BANDWIDTH.

business graphics : The market segment associated with the graphical display of business data, encompassing bar charts, pie charts, and the like.

button *n.* 1 : A mechanical button, as on a mouse, providing a discrete input to a computer. 2 : A representation of a button on a graphics display, typically selected by positioning a cursor over the button and actuating with a mouse or other selection device.

byte *n.* : Eight bits grouped as a unit for storage and processing. In early computing, a byte corresponded to the unit needed to store a character, and there were computers with six, seven, and nine bit bytes; but anything other than eight is now uncommon. —Compare OCTET.

byte addressability : —See ADDRESSABILITY.

C

C [originated by D. Ritchie during the development of UNIX as a successor to K. Thompson's language "B," which in turn derived from a language called BCPL, *Basic Combined Programming Language*] *n.* : Programming language closely associated with the UNIX operating system, now widely used by professional programmers. The language is capable of providing especially concise and efficient code, at the potential risk of being obscure.

C++ : Variant of the C programming language including extended features to support object-oriented programming. C and C++ are the dominant programming languages for graphics and virtual reality applications.

C3 *C-3*\\ [*alt.* C^3, C-cubed] [military jargon] : Functions related to military command, control, and communications.

C4 *C-4*\\ [*alt.* C^4] : CAD, CAM, CAE, CIM; the disciplines related to the use of computers and computer graphics to automate design and production processes.

C30 : The TMS320C30 digital signal-processing chip produced by Texas Instruments and used in a number of graphics products. The family of TMS320Cx0 products presents a variety of signal-processing capabilities.

cab *n.* : The portion of a simulator that houses the users, such as a physical mock-up of an aircraft cockpit or other vehicle interior.

cache *cash*\\ *n.* : Local high-speed storage designed to provide quick access to frequently used data also stored in a larger, slower memory.

cache coherency *n.* : Keeping of data values consistent in a cache and the larger memory the cache mirrors.

CAD *cad*\\ : Computer-Aided Design; the broad application area involving the application of computers, and usually computer graphics, to the solution of engineering design problems.

CAD/CAM *cad cam*\\ [*alt.* CADCAM] : Computer-Aided Design and Computer-Aided Manufacturing; the encompassing term for virtually all computer and computer graphics applications related to the design and manufacturing of products.

CADD : Computer-Aided Drafting and Design; computer graphics applications to design activities that traditionally involved hand drawing, such as the preparation of mechanical drawings or electrical schematics.

18

CADDS : Computer-*A*ided *D*rafting and *D*esign *S*ystem(s); a particular set of hardware and software used for CADD activities.

CAD-E : Computer-*A*ided *D*esign and *E*ngineering

CAD-M : Computer-*A*ided *D*esign and *M*anufacturing.

CAE : Computer-*A*ided *E*ngineering; use of computers and computer graphics to facilitate engineering design activities. Often prefaced by the branch of engineering, for example, *mechanical CAE.*

CAI : Computer-*A*ided *I*nstruction; use of computers and computer graphics to facilitate teaching.

calligraphic display : A type of CRT display in which lines are drawn by directing the beam of the display in x-y coordinates; now largely supplanted by raster graphics displays. : STROKE DISPLAY.

candela *n.* : A unit of luminous intensity, i.e., the amount of light per unit solid angle from a point source, equal to one lumen per steradian.

candidate list : In ray tracing, a list of graphics objects determined to be likely to intersect a given ray.

canvas [NeWS terminology] *n.* : WINDOW.

carrier *n.* : In electrostatic printing technology, a substance that conveys or disperses a toner without toning the image itself.

Cartesian coordinates [occasionally not cap.] : The common isometric coordinate system in which the location of a point is specified by an ordered set of distances corresponding to the point's projection on each of the mutually perpendicular coordinate axes : rectangular coordinates : x,y coordinates (for two dimensions) : x,y,z coordinates (for three dimensions).

CASE : Computer-*A*ided *S*oftware *E*ngineering; workstation application area encompassing the development of programs to aid the design and development of application programs. Although this includes the broad variety of software tools, such as editors, compilers, and debuggers, CASE is sometimes used with special reference to design and analysis tools having an interactive graphical interface.

cathode ray tube : —See CRT.

Catmull-Rom spline : A type of spline, useful in graphics modeling, that interpolates, i.e., it passes through its control points.

CAV : Constant *A*ngular *V*elocity; a format for optical disk recording of video signals in which the same number of video frames are recorded on each revolution of the disk over the whole recording surface, even though constant data density would allow more near the outer edge. Having the data aligned by angle over the disk facilitates special effects like freeze frame and slow motion. —Compare CLV.

CCD : Charge-Coupled Device; a semiconductor device configured in shift-register arrays for sensing light. Used in some television cameras and scanners.

CCITT \C-C-I-T-T\ : Consultative Committee for International Telephone and Telegraphy; international committee setting standards related to communications, including compressed video transmission and computer networks.

CD-ROM : Compact Disk Read Only Memory; an interchangeable digital storage media having data encoded optically on a disk for readback by a laser in a drive that rotates the disk. The technology is similar to disks used for digital audio recordings, but encoded differently.

cel [*alt.* cell] *n.* 1 : Method of animation in which art is drawn on transparent material so that successive images may be overlaid on fixed background artwork. 2 : In computer graphics, especially flight simulation, a pattern of an image including both color and transparency values for each pixel that is mapped as a texture into a scene. Typical uses are for tree foliage, smoke effects, and clouds.

cell *n.* 1 : In graphics standards including GKS and PHIGS, a rectangular element, not necessarily in correspondence with a pixel, whose only nongeometric property is its color. 2 : In an alphanumeric raster display having fixed character spacing, one of the blocks of pixels, each in a fixed position, in which a character or symbol may be displayed.

cell array : A GKS primitive similar to a raster.

center of projection : VIEWPOINT.

CGA : Computer Graphics Adapter; an IBM-originated design and inter-face standard for a personal computer color frame buffer providing 200 x 320 resolution. Now obsolesced by higher-resolution standards.

CGI 1 : Computer Generated Imagery; images generated using computer graphics techniques, especially real-time imagery for flight simulation or cockpit displays. 2 : Computer Graphics Interface; an ANSI/ISO standard under development for direct communication of drawing primitives to graphics devices. Previously called **Virtual Device Metafile.**

CGM : Computer Graphics Metafile; an ANSI standard that provides a format for exchanging pictorial two-dimensional information, typically for devices like plotters.

character *n.* 1 : A predefined code, typically eight bits, representing a symbol or a control function. **Displayable characters** correspond to symbols including alphanumerics that may be displayed or printed. **Control characters** usually are not displayed but are interpreted to initiate or alter processing operations. 2 : The symbol corresponding to a character code.

character field : The rectangular region within which a character may be displayed.

character generator : Hardware dedicated to rendering predefined characters on a display device.

character graphics : Simple graphics imagery generated by using predefined graphics characters stored as a font. The most common example is the use of characters representing the single and double lines with their horizontal and vertical intersections, used for drawing boxes and the like.

character spacing : A text attribute specifying, usually as a fraction of character height, the space to be added between successive character fields.

charge-coupled device : —See CCD.

child raster : A data object that designates a rectangular area of either screen or nonscreen memory, depending upon the type of its parent raster.

chip [from the small piece of semiconductor material in the device] *n.* : An integrated circuit device. The semiconductor material itself, exclusive of the packaging, is referred to as the **die**, *pl.* **dice**.

choice device : In GKS, a logical input providing an integer indicating which of a set of alternatives has been selected.

Christmas tree effect [*slang*] : The tendency to add features to a product over time : **creeping featurism.**

chroma *n.* : The hue and saturation components of color, exclusive of the brightness. Also, **chromatic** *adj.* : relating to the chroma.

chroma control : The control on a monitor that adjusts color saturation.

chroma keying [*alt.* chromakeying] : COLOR KEYING.

chromaticity coordinates : TRISTIMULUS COORDINATES.

chromaticity diagram : A plot of the (x,y) portion of xyY color space.

chrominance *n.* : The part of a composite color video signal that carries the hue and saturation information, while the luminance part of the signal carries the brightness information. —See also, YIQ.

CI : —See COMMAND INTERFACE.

CIE \C-I-E\ : Commission International L'Eclairage; international committee that has established a standard means for specifying the color of an object or light source in terms of *tristimulus* coordinates.

CIELAB [Commission International L'Eclairage + Lightness + *a**, *b** axis labels] [*alt.* CIE (L* a* b*)] : A standardized color space providing approximately equal steps of perceived color change for equal changes in coordinate values. The space is in cylindrical coordinates in the style of the Munsell space. A second, different, approximation has also been standardized, the **CIELUV** space.

CIELUV [*alt.* CIE (L* u* v*)] : —See CIELAB.

CIE XYZ : —See XYZ SPACE.

CIM : Computer-*Integrated* *Manufacturing*; the application of computers to the maintaining of manufacturing databases and the control of production.

cine mode : Rapid sequencing through a series of digital images on a display to provide an animation, especially in the context of medical imaging.

circular addressing : CIRCULAR BUFFERING.

circular buffering *n.* : A memory-addressing scheme used to keep a sequence of data in which values first entered are subsequently first removed. Pointers for the start and end of the received data queue are compared with the boundaries of the allocated memory space, and out-of-bounds addresses, which would result from advancing a pointer, are mapped back to the start of the allocated space. If too much data are enqueued, the start and end pointers will overlap, resulting in a (usually cryptically noted) circular buffer error. : CIRCULAR ADDRESSING. —Compare FIFO.

CISC \rhymes with *risk*\ : Complex *Instruction* *Set* Computer; a computer processor having instructions typically requiring more than one or two clock cycles to execute. —Compare RISC.

class : A collection of graphics objects having the same type of attributes and to which the same types of operators apply.

classification : A technique in ray tracing whereby rays are grouped by origin, direction, or other characteristic with the objective of improving processing efficiency.

client 1 : One of the programs using a window system to share graphics resources. 2 : More generally, any process that accesses either a graphics library or a graphics server. 3: Any computer using the services of a network.

clip art [closely analogous to traditional printed books of images used by the publishing trade] : A digital image or graphics data file sold in collections of such images or files, for incorporation into a user's publication.

clip boundary : A set of planes defining a region in three dimensions, outside of which graphics objects are eliminated from rendering by clipping.

clip path : A two-dimensional boundary, often maintained as a list of line segments in virtual device coordinates, to which displayable graphics objects are clipped.

clipping *n.* 1 : The process of altering the boundaries of graphics primitives so that none extend beyond a prescribed region (or regions). Commonly, clipping is performed so that a computed image is constrained to the boundaries of a display or a region in a window on the display. 2 : In the processing of video signals, applying a limit to the amplitude of black, white, or synchronization signals, or some combination of the three.

clip rectangle : A rectangle in virtual device coordinates to which displayable graphics objects are clipped.

clip region [*alt.* clipping region] : In a window system, the portions of a window outside of which output is to be removed by clipping. The clip region may be defined by a clip path, a set of rectangles, a bitmap, or other means.

clip test : Any relatively quick test, such as checking a bounding box, to see if a graphics primitive or group of graphics data is entirely within a clipping region. If the data are entirely within the region, it need not be clipped, if they are entirely outside the region, it is discarded, and if they are neither entirely within or without, it is subject to more precise tests or to clipping algorithms. The objective is to save overall processing time. —See HULL, BUBBLE TEST.

closure *n.* : The accuracy with which lines intended to meet at a point actually meet; of particular interest for calligraphic graphics systems.

clubby *adj.* : With respect to an image produced by electrostatic printing, having reduced sharpness or definition. Also, *n.* : **clubbiness.**

cluster *n.* 1 : A group of convex graphics objects linearly separable from other such groups; i.e., so that a nonintersecting plane may be passed between any two clusters. —See SCHUMACHER ALGORITHM. 2 : More generally, any set of graphics objects grouped for convenience in a database hierarchy. —Compare SEGMENT.

CLV : *Constant Linear Velocity*; a format for optical disk recording of video signals in which the same density of data is maintained over the whole recording *surface* of the disk, yielding the longest playing time per disk. —Compare CAV.

CMAP : *Color Map*; a data object defining the color model for a raster.

CMOS *see-moss*, rarely *cosmos*\ : Complimentary Metal-Oxide Semiconductor; a popular technology used for manufacturing integrated circuits, using both p-type and n-type transistors. Characterized by negligible power consumption when idle, but power rising in proportion to the operating frequency.

CMYK : *Cyan, Magenta, Yellow, Key* [*key* is used for black so as to avoid the *b*, which could be confused as signifying *blue*]; the color space used for printing, black being added to provide extra contrast as compared with what can be obtained by overprinting the other three colors.

codec \co-deck\ [*alt.* CODEC] *n.* : *Coder-decoder*; a pair of devices for compressing data by encoding it and subsequently reconstructing the data by decoding it, usually in the context of a communications system in which compression is performed to conserve bandwidth. For example, a codec used for video teleconferencing.

coherence *n.* : The tendency of adjacent pixels or scanlines, or successive frames of an animated sequence, to have similar color, occlusion priority, or relative motion. A number of graphics algorithms exploit coherence as a way of minimizing processing time or conserving storage space. Also, **coherency** *adj.* : exhibiting coherence.

colinear *adj.* : With respect to two or more points, lying on the same line.

collimated *n.* : Optically focused so as to provide an image that appears to be at infinity, for example, with reference to display optics for flight simulators. This is done to enhance the realism of the simulation display, but it incidentally produces an image with minimum eye strain since the eye muscles are relaxed for focus at infinity. Also, *adj.* : being **collimated**; **collimate** *v.t.* : to cause to become collimated; **collimator** *n.* : a device for collimating.

collision detection *n.* : Detection, through the use of computer algorithms, of the contact or interpenetration of mathematically described three-dimensional models, usually for the purpose of aiding a model of physical interaction. For example, an animation of an image of a ball bouncing on a surface will require detection of the collision of the ball with the surface, otherwise the ball would pass right through the surface.

color *n.* : The class of phenomena related to the human observation and scientific measurements of energy at frequencies in the visible portion of the electromagnetic spectrum, including how humans perceive different spectra and how materials selectively absorb and reflect the spectra. While instruments measure many variations of energies in narrow bands over the spectra of light from objects, human vision has been found to distinguish only three basic characteristics. One way to summarize the three characteristics is as hue, saturation, and value, but there are other equally valid *color spaces*. —See HSV SPACE, CIE COORDINATES, METAMER.

color burst : In a composite video signal for color television, a series of cycles of the chrominance subcarrier used to synchronize the color oscillator in the display system.

color edging : A line of incorrect color along one or more edges of an object in a graphics image : —See FRINGING.

colorimetry : The scientific study of the human perception of colors, especially from the viewpoint of quantitative measurement.

colorizing *n.* 1 : Pseudocoloring. 2 : Adding color to a black-and-white movie through a combination of artistic and computer means. Also, **colorize** *v.t.* : to perform colorizing.

color keying : A way of combining two images in which the presence of a certain color in one image is used as the signal to include the corresponding part of the other image. In video applications, a blue-green background in one image is often used to trigger inclusion of a background image from a different source.

color model 1 : The format used to store color information in a frame buffer, for example. an eight-bit indexed color model or a 24-bit true-color model. 2 : The method used to specify colors for a graphics system, such as the coordinates in a specified color space.

color purity : —See PURITY.

color space 1 : The set of colors made available to a graphics application by a graphics system. 2 : Any of the many different coordinate systems used to represent some or all of the full range of visible colors.

color table : A look-up table, usually embedded in hardware, for translating color index numbers into red, blue, and green color components.

COM *comm*\ *n.* : Computer Output Microfilm; a computer peripheral device producing alphanumeric or graphical output directly on microfilm, or the computer print or graphics so written.

COMDEX : *Computer Dealers Exposition*; annual exposition for the personal computer industry.

command interface : The document describing the format and use of instructions driving a hardware device (typically a graphics accelerator).

command stream : A sequence of control information passed from one processor to another.

comparitor *n.* 1 : Circuit element comparing two binary values and producing a control signal output indicating whether they are equal or unequal. 2: Circuit element comparing two fixed or floating point values and producing an output indicating the cases of whether one is greater, less than, or equal to the other.

compensation table [less common] : GAMMA CORRECTION TABLE.

compilation *n.* : Preprocessing of a display list (or leaf) to convert graphics commands and data from a general format into a hardware-specific format. Also, **compile** *v.t.* : to perform compilation upon.

complementary colors : A pair of colors opposite each other in a polar-coordinate hue space, such as the Munsell system.

Complementary Metal-Oxide Semiconductor : —See CMOS

composite sync : A synchronization signal for raster scanned video in which the elements for horizontal (scanline) and. vertical (field) synchronization have been added to form a single signal. Composite sync is used with either *composite* or *RGB* video.

composite video : A video signal format in which the elements describing color, brightness, and synchronization are combined so that the signal may, for example, be sent on a single wire. All of the television standards are for composite video. —See RGB VIDEO.

compositing *n.* : The combining of two or more separately prepared images into one, usually through pixel-by-pixel transparency (*or alpha*) computation, and sometimes with z comparison. Also, **composite** *v.t.* : to perform compositing; *adj.* : being composited; *n.* : the result of compositing.

compression *n.* : Processing a file or stream of data to reduce the amount of data to be stored or transferred by encoding redundant information. *Reversible* compression techniques allow decompression back to a form bit-for-bit identical with the original data. Techniques that are not reversible yield approximations to the original data, as, for example, for stored imagery, and generally allow higher compression ratios. Typically, reversible compression reduces a data file by 2 : 1, and nonreversible compression for imagery by about 12 : 1. Special circumstances, such as time sequences of similar images, may yield much higher compression ratios. Also, **compress** *v.t.* : to perform compression.

computer-aided design : —See CAD.

computer-aided design/computer-aided manufacturing : —See CAD/ CAM.

computer-aided drafting and design : —See CADD.

computer-aided engineering : —See CAE.

computer-aided instruction : —See CAI.

computer-aided manufacturing : —See CAM.

computer-aided software engineering : —See CASE.

computer generated imagery : —See CGI [1].

computer graphics : The processes associated with producing images by digital rendering of a modeled database. Digital processing is always performed, but all or part of the processing may be done with specialized hardware, and not necessarily with a general-purpose computer. The output may be to a stroke or raster CRT display, to a printer or plotter, or to any of a variety of other display devices.

Computer Graphics Adapter : —See CGA.

Computer Graphics Interface : —See CGI [2].

Computer Graphics Metafile : —See CGM.

computer-integrated manufacturing : —See CIM.

computer output microfilm : —See COM.

Computervision : Bedford, MA, company, a major producer of MCAD systems now a division of Prime Computers, Inc.

concave polygon : A polygon having at least one interior angle greater than 180 degrees.

cone tracing : A variation of ray tracing using conical regions rather than single rays of light, with the objective of reducing the total computation required.

configuration *n.* : The set of hardware elements, including the graphics and storage options, making up a particular computer system. More generally, including the software elements.

Constant Angular Velocity : —See CAV.

Constant Linear Velocity : —See CLV.

constant shading : FLAT SHADING.

constructive solid geometry : —See CSG.

context *n.* 1 : A complete collection of all the values of the state variables associated with a given set of conditions in a graphics processing pipeline. 2 : A data object that holds graphics rendering state information as a set of attributes.

continuous picking : —See PICKING.

contour *n.* : A curve giving the locus of points where a continuous function is equal to a given constant. The contours on a map are the curves of equal elevation of the terrain.

contrast *n.* 1 : The ratio of the maximum to the minimum intensity in an image or display. For a CRT display, the maximum luminance of the display is compared with the amount of environmental light reflected from the unlit phosphor. Sometimes a further distinction is made between **range contrast**, measured from the brightest area of the display to the dimmest, and **detail contrast**, measured between nearby pixels and limited by internal reflections. —See also, DYNAMIC RANGE. 2 : The change in output intensity relative to input intensity in a display or image-producing system. Higher contrast corresponds to more rapid transitions from black to white in the output.

contrast threshold function : —See CTF.

control point [*alt.* control vertex] : One of a set of points in space used as parameters for a curve or curved surface. For geometric modeling, the control points are adjusted to shape the curve as desired. Depending upon the type of curve, the curve may or may not pass through the control points.

convergence *n.* : The superimposing of the three colors in a color CRT display.

convergence error : Failure of the three colors in a CRT display to be correctly registered with respect to each other, typically resulting in color fringes on the edges of white portions of the image.

convex *adj.* : For a geometric figure, having the property that any two points within the figure may be connected by a straight line lying entirely within the figure.

convolution *n.* : Application of a convolution integral to a set of data. For sampled digital data this amounts to computing an output data set from an input data set by computing each point in the output as a weighted sum of the neighboring input data values. The set of weights is fixed and forms the *convolution kernel*. Commonly for image processing, each pixel in an output image is computed as the weighted sum of input image pixels in a block around the output pixel address. In that case, the weights forming the kernel are conveniently represented by a matrix. Also, **convolve** *v.t.* : to perform convolution with.

convolution kernel *n.* : In the context of antialiasing for computer graphics, the function describing how the energy from a theoretically infinitely concentrated point of light would be spread for addition to pixels containing and neighboring the point. The antialiased image for display is conceptually built by summing the scaled contributions of the kernels associated with all the points in the underlying image, via a convolution integral. In practice, tables or approximation techniques are used to find the contributions to be added to pixels in the neighborhood of a pixel covered by portions of a line or a polygon. —See also, BOX FILTER.

convolver *n.* : In image processing, hardware dedicated to performing convolution on an image.

Convolvotron™ [apparently from *convolution*, a method of digital filtering] *n.* : a device for creating high-fidelity three-dimensional sound in real time, produced by Crystal River Engineering.

Coons patch : A surface fitted to four arbitrary boundary curves.

coplanar *adj.* : With respect to two or more points, lines, line segments, or polygons, lying in the same plane.

coprocessor *n.* : A second processor sharing computations or other processing tasks in a computer system, especially one that performs a specialized set of processes such as a **math coprocessor** that performs floating point arithmetic.

corotron [from *corona*] *n.* : An electrostatic charging device used in a copying machine or electrostatic printer.

cracking *n.* : The creation of unintended gaps between polygons intended to share edges, typically as a result of round-off errors or slight algorithmic inconsistencies. —See also, PATCH CRACKING, EDGE MERGING.

Cracking

crawling *n.* : An aliasing artifact in which an edge in a sequence of graphics images appears to move discretely from one scanline (or column of pixels) to the next, rather than moving smoothly. If the effect is apparent on both edges of an object a few pixels wide, the object will appear to significantly change in width as it moves. Also, **crawl** *v.i.* : to exhibit crawling.

creeping featurism [*slang*] : The tendency to add features to a product over time : **Christmas tree effect**.

critical fusion frequency : The display refresh rate at which flicker disappears, a function of the display angular size, the display brightness, and the individual observer. The lowest frequency used is about 50 Hz (PAL television) and the highest about 76 Hz (new European standards for VDTs).

critical path : In project management, the contingent sequence of tasks in a project plan that places a lower bound on the time required to accomplish a project, so that any increase in the duration of tasks on the critical path will accordingly lengthen the minimum schedule. The critical path is only defined under circumstances in which resources (like manpower) are not the limiting factor. (If resources are the limitation, then increasing or decreasing the duration of any resource-limited task will have an effect on the total schedule.)

cropping *n.* : Editing an image by selecting a portion of the image for retention and removing the rest. Also, **crop** *v.t.* : to perform cropping upon.

cross-hairs *n.* : A type of graphics cursor consisting of horizontal and vertical lines that intersect at the position currently selected. The horizontal and vertical lines extend over the full dimensions of the screen or, in the case of an application in a window, over the full dimensions of the viewport.

cross-hatch *v.t.* : To fill a region with cross-hatching.

cross-hatching *n.* : A pattern composed of uniformly spaced parallel lines intersected, typically perpendicularly, by similar lines in a similar pattern.

CRT : Cathode Ray Tube; common element for displays, using a beam of electrons, electrostatically or electromagnetically deflected, to excite a phosphor on the inner surface of a glass faceplate of an evacuated tube. The electrons originate from a heated metal cathode and are electrically focused into a beam and accelerated. The CRT is one element of a *CRT display* or *monitor* also having a case, chassis, power supply, and control electronics.

CRU : Customer Replaceable Unit; a component or subassembly of a device that is designed for replacement by the customer when service is required.

CrystalEyes™ [presumably from *liquid crystal eyewear*] *n.* : stereo viewing glasses manufactured by StereoGraphics, Inc., in which liquid crystal shutter devices open and close electronically so that each eye sees only the intended alternate images on a direct view or projected display.

CSG : Constructive Solid Geometry; a solid modeling method using the Boolean intersection of primitive objects to define general models. For example, an object having a hole might be modeled by subtracting a cylindrical model of the hole from the solid object. —Compare B-REP.

CTF : Contrast Threshold Function; the minimum perceptible contrast for a specific observer of a display, as a function of spatial frequency.

CT scanner : Computed Tomography scanner; a device producing data for medical imaging using a low-intensity X-ray source and an array of typically more than 700 detectors. By rotating the source and detector array the system can compute a cross-sectional image of the subject.

cuberille *adj.* : Of or related to a model used for the visualization of three-dimensional data in which space is subdivided into equal-sized rectangular volumes, and, for rendering, polygonal faces are constructed for selected volumes depending upon the data values in each volume. The faces are consolidated, using various techniques, to improve rendering speed.

culling *n.* : The elimination of data from graphics processing by subjecting it to relatively simple tests, such as whether the entire object is behind the plane of the observer or whether a particular polygon is backfacing. Also, **cull** *v.t.* : to perform culling upon.

culture *n.* 1 : The set of man-made features such as roads, buildings, power lines, and the like, as data for representation on a map. 2 : In flight simulation graphics, the set of man-made features represented by graphics models in a simulation database. Sometimes more broadly defined to include all the elements of a database except for the modeled terrain.

cursor *n.* 1 : A graphics icon, marker, or cross-hairs used to point to an object or position on the screen, typically positioned under the control of an input device and superimposed over all other graphics imagery. 2 : The movable part of a digitizer tablet, usually a stylus or puck.

cursor planes *n.* : Memory space (typically two bits) associated with each pixel used to store the data for a superimposed cursor, allowing large or complex cursor patterns to be drawn without interfering with the memory holding the underlying imagery.

curve segment : A portion of a curve lying between two predefined points.

Customer Replaceable Unit : —See CRU.

CUT : The file extension used to designate bit-mapped image files in the format produced by the personal computer paint program *Dr. Halo,* and related programs.

cut plane : SECTION PLANE.

cuts and jumps : Modifications to a printed circuit assembly made by cutting board traces and adding jumper wires to effect circuit changes; used extensively while debugging prototype boards, but some small number is typically allowed in production.

CV : —See COMPUTERVISION.

cyan *n.* : One of the primary colors of color printing; approximately blue-green. Also, *adj.* : cyan-colored.

cyber- [*Prefix* from *cybernetics*] : virtual reality related.

cyberia [*slang*] *n.* : Cyberspace.

cybernaut *n.* : 1. A person who explores a simulated environment using an immersive virtual reality system. 2. Any practitioner of virtual reality.

cybernetics [coined by Norbert Wiener, 1948, fr. Gk. *kybernetes*, pilot] *n.* : science of communication automatic control, esp. in comparison to the mechanisms of the brain and nervous system; not closely related to most of the enterprises to which the *cyber-* prefix is now attached.

cyberpunk [coined by science fiction author Gardner Dozois] *n.* : A countercultural style including punk and science fiction themes. An extended discussion of cyberpunk is contained in Francis Hamit's book *Virtual Reality and the Exploration of Cyberspace,* SAMS Publishing, 1993, ISBN 0-672-30361-1, pp. 294-295.

cybersex *n.* : Teledildonics, although perhaps cybersex is a more genteel term.

cyberspace [possibly the virtual reality term now in broadest general use] *n.* 1 : Computer equipment, software, data, and communications viewed as a world unto itself with which humans interact. 2 : A virtual environment, especially as defined by the database of objects in the environment. 3 : Computer systems or technology that is used for direct interaction with humans.

cyclic overlap : The arrangement of a set of graphics objects such that they cannot be placed in an occlusion (or *priority*) order such that higher-priority objects strictly occlude lower-priority objects.

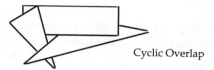

Cyclic Overlap

cylinder primitive : A graphics primitive sought by molecular modeling users to represent the bonds between atoms; often used with an orthographic rendering.

D

D1 *D one*\ *n.* : A format for encoding a video signal as a sequence of binary numbers having eight bits per pixel.

D2 *D two*\ *n.* : A format for encoding a video signal as a sequence of binary numbers having 10 bits per pixel.

DAC *dack*\ *n.* 1 [*alt.* D/A converter] : Digital-to-Analog Converter; a circuit element that converts digital data, such as the color values stored in a frame buffer, into time-varying analog signals such as the display video sent to a monitor. 2 : Design Automation Conference, the major conference for producers and users of CADDS and other design-related tools.

daemon *n.* : A program that executes continually on a computer system to handle network administration, print spooling, and the like.

Dash Gates™ : A logic design tool including a Boolean equation compiler, truth table compiler, state machine compiler, and logic optimizer; mainly for the preparation of PALs.

database [*alt.* data base] 1 : The entire set of graphics objects available on-line for rendering by a graphics system as applied by a user. The database is usually stored on disk and includes nongraphics information as well as graphics data. 2 : In the broader context, any set of data available on-line.

database coordinates : The common coordinate system of a graphics database : MODEL COORDINATES.

data dictionary : A dictionary of the data items used on a project, associating variable names with formats and descriptions, used to guarantee consistent usage over the project.

data glove *n.* : An instrumented glove worn for providing the positions and orientations of the hand and fingers as inputs to a computer.

DataGlove™ [VPL Research, Inc.] *n.* : A computer input device worn as a glove that provides data for finger position and flex.

dataless *adj.* : Of a computer on a network, having its own disk storage and basic software, but relying upon the network server for booting and other services.

dataspace *n.* 1 : Cyberspace. 2 : A cyberspace used to accomplish data visualization.

DataSuit *n.* : VPL Research pioneering brand of bodysuit.

34

data tablet : DIGITIZER : TABLET.

data visualization *n.* : Process by which engineering, scientific, financial, or other data are represented as a graphics image, usually as a perspective image and often presented interactively from varying viewpoints.

DCT *D-C-T*\\ : *Discrete Cosine Transform;* the mathematical basis of widely used image compression algorithms in which blocks of pixels are characterized by spatial frequencies. The frequency components having small coefficients are removed in the compression process.

DDA *D-D-A*\\ : *Digital Differential Analyzer;* an algorithm for rasterizing a line or curve by recursively applying the slope of the line to a unit raster step and rounding to the nearest pixel.

DDES™ : *Digital Data Exchange Standard;* a magnetic tape format for supplying digital images in the CMYK color space for offset printing.

deallocate *v.t.* : To release a shared resource, such as memory or table space, to make it available to other processes or applications.

deassert *v.t.* : To change a binary electronic control signal from the state that initiates action back to its idle state.

debounce *v.t.* : To condition the signal from a mechanical switch closure so that a single transition occurs for each actuation, suppressing the multiple short pulses that may occur due to the mechanism not opening or closing cleanly.

DEC™ *deck*\\: *Digital Equipment Corp.,* Maynard, MA; major producer of minicomputer systems and workstations.

deck [*slang,* possibly from *tape deck,* a tape player, or possibly from *Holodeck,* a science fiction conception of VR apparatus] *n.* : An equipment set for generating virtual reality experiences, especially the concept of appliance-like equipment that is self-contained and easy to use.

declutter *v.t.* : To remove overlayed imagery, such as symbols overlayed on a terrain map or extra symbology in an aircraft head-up display.

DECnet™ *deck-net*\\ : Proprietary networking system for DEC computers.

decoder *n.* 1 : A device that reconstructs compressed imagery or other compressed data. 2 : Circuitry that separates the red, green, and blue components of an input composite video signal. 3 : Software routine, usually resident in a graphics device, which translates commands from a system interface into a sequence of hardware-specific instructions used within the device.

deep *adj.* : Having high color saturation and low color value, i.e., being comparatively pure and dark in color.

degauss *v.t.* : To remove the magnetization from an object, in particular to remove the magnetism from the shadowmask of a CRT so as to eliminate local color impurities caused by the magnetic distortions. The shadowmask can become magnetized by long term orientation with the earth's magnetic field or by a strong local magnetic field, such as produced by starting an electric motor. Most CRT displays now have a built-in coil around the faceplate to facilitate automatic degaussing whenever the display is powered up.

de-iconify *v.t.* : —See ICONIFY.

depth buffer : Z-BUFFER.

depth complexity *n.* : The number of pixels or fractional pixel contributions that must be generated in the preparation divided by the number that appears in the final image. The depth complexity of most images is greater than one because pixels are occluded and fractional pixel contributions are needed for antialiasing and transparent objects.

depth cueing : Interpolation of a graphics object's color and intensity to that of a predetermined background as a function of distance. If the background is black, this amounts to reducing the intensity of the object with distance. —See also, LINEAR DEPTH CUEING, FADING.

depth perception *n.* : The ability to judge the distance of objects usually through the use of stereo vision, but more generally through cues such as perspective, relative motion, occlusion, and atmospheric haze effects.

design rule checking : —See DRC.

deskside *adj.* : Too large to fit on the top of an office desk, but small enough to fit within the confines of an average office, particularly with reference to a workstation.

desktop *adj.* 1: Small enough to fit on the top of an office desk, particularly a computer or computer system. 2 : Intended to be performed with a system that fits in an office environment rather than with more specialized equipment, although not necessarily literally on a desk top, <desktop publishing>. Also, *n.* : The graphics image of an office desk top as used by computer programs as a user interface, typically featuring icons for documents, folders, and the like.

Desktop Bus : Apple Computer bus for connecting graphics input devices such as joysticks, tablets, and the like.

desktop publishing : Publishing activities performed with a personal computer and peripherals, rather than with traditional typography and paste-up methods.

detail contrast : —See CONTRAST.

device coordinates : A coordinate system for graphics defined in the hardware of a graphics processor, display system, or peripheral device, such as the coordinates associated with a digitizing tablet.

device-dependent : Using a property of a specific implementation, particularly in the context of standard graphics software ported to different graphics hardware. For example, the number of displayable colors is likely to be device dependent. Opposite of **device-independent.**

device driver : A routine within operating system software dedicated to the control of attached hardware such as a disk storage unit or graphics accelerator.

device space : The set of addressable or readable coordinates associated with a graphics output or input device.

DFD \D-F-D\ : Data Flow Diagram; a diagram showing the flow of data among processes and data stores, developed as an aid to the analysis and design of systems.

DGIS : A standard interface for personal computer graphics, precursor of *TIGA.*

dial box : A computer input device providing two or more dials and knobs for general purpose, typically graphics-related, applications.

dials and knobs : Computer input devices that have rotating settings, providing quantitative inputs corresponding to rotational position; the interpretation of the inputs is usually programmed for each application. A typical application uses the dials to set the rotational angles or position coordinates of a graphics object, such as a molecular model.

die *n.* : —See CHIP.

DIF *diff*\ : Drawing Interchange Format; the graphics object-oriented format used by the program *AutoCAD* and other CAD drawing programs. Also used as the file extension, DIF, for files in that format.

difference *n.* : In constructive solid geometry, the region in three-dimensional space within one or the other of two specified solid objects, but not within both.

differential pulse-code modulation : —See DPCM.

Digital Data Exchange Standard : —See DDES.

digital differential analyzer : —See DDA.

Digital Equipment Corp. : —See DEC.

digital halftoning : —See DITHERING.

digital-to-analog converter : —See DAC.

digital video 1 : A video signal encoded as a sequence of binary numbers, especially in D1 or D2. 2 : The technology of generating, recording, and processing digital video signals.

Digital Video Interactive : —See DVI.

digitize *v.t.* : To measure and record properties of real-world objects or other data in a digital format, especially the shape of an object or the light variation in an image.

digitizer *n.* : A graphics input device comprising a drawing-board–like instrumented flat surface and a movable puck having a cursor, for entering the coordinates of points off drawings by selecting them with the puck. A similar device using a stylus instead of a puck is called a *data tablet* (or *tablet)*, although sometimes the various terms are used interchangeably. Three-dimensional digitizers typically use a stylus to select points within a prescribed volume.

dingbat *n.* : In typography, a nonalphanumeric symbol of a size similar to a letter or number, such as a small circle, pointing hand, square, or arrow.

directional light : A light source that radiates nonuniformly in space, as, for example, a spotlight.

direction cube : A cube centered at the origin of a rectangular coordinate system with coordinate axes passing through the center of each face, used to represent directions in space by the point of intersection of a line from the origin with the cube. The six faces of the cube may be mapped into two dimensions, with rectangular subdivisions of the cube map corresponding to subdivisions of the directions in space. This means of subdividing directions in space is useful for a number of ray-tracing algorithms.

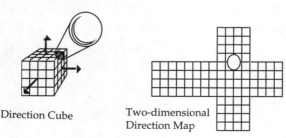

Direction Cube

Two-dimensional
Direction Map

direct port : In a graphics accelerator, the hardware interface that bypasses the accelerator to permit direct reading and writing into the frame buffer.

direct user : A graphics system user who renders to graphics devices through a local copy of a low-level graphics language, usually for maximum performance.

direct view storage tube : —See DVST.

DIS *dis*\\: *D*istributed *I*nteractive *S*imulation; a simulation performed over a network in which players appear in each other's displays according to data passed in a military-originated standard format.

discrete *n.* 1 : An electronic component having a single circuit element such as a resistor, capacitor, or transistor; or at most a low level of circuit integration, such as an SSI package. Also, *adj.* : Being built of discrete components, the opposite of *integrated*.

discrete cosine transform : —See DCT.

diskfull *adj.* : Having a local disk storage memory unit.

diskless *adj.* : Not having a local disk storage memory unit, usually with reference to a networked workstation.

display *n.* : A device for presenting data to human senses, traditionally a visual display, but now occasionally used more generally for touch or the other senses, such as a *force display*.

displayable *adj.* : Being within the capabilities of a particular display device, such as being within the color gamut of the display.

displayable character : —See CHARACTER.

display buffer : Memory for storing a display list : —See also, **display file.**

display device : The component in a display system that converts signals into a visible image, for example, a cathode ray tube.

display element : A *graphics primitive*, especially in the context of primitives rendered by specialized hardware driving a display.

display file : A display list kept in a file.

display list : A list of graphics commands and data built-in memory for subsequent rendering and display. The list may be hierarchical with embedded control elements determining what commands and data should be selected for display. —See also, TRAVERSAL.

display order : An instruction for a graphics accelerator.

display parameters : Color look-up tables and other information that indicates how the pixel information is to be displayed.

display surface : The medium upon which a displayed image is written, such as paper or CRT phosphors.

display system : A system including signal-processing circuitry and a display device for displaying imagery.

display writer : The instrument drawing a displayed image, such as a pen, cutting stylus, or electron beam.

dissolve *v.t.* : To change between two images or sequences of images by adding the two with a proportion that is constant over the image and uniformly changing in time. Used, for example, to transition between scenes in film or video work. Also, *n.* : the sequence created by dissolving.

distributed graphics : Division of a graphics process into subtasks for execution on separate processors, especially on networked computers. One motivation is to permit complex graphics computations to be performed by a specialized high-performance processor that can be accessed by simpler display terminals over a network.

Distributed Interactive Simulation : —See DIS.

distributed ray tracing : Execution of a ray-tracing algorithm concurrently on separate processors through subdivision of the processing tasks into subtasks, assignment of the subtasks to processors, and subsequent collection and integration of the results. The high computational demands of ray tracing together with the relative ease of dividing the task into independent subtasks makes this application of special interest.

dithering [originally used in engineering for noise deliberately added to a control loop] *n.* : Adding pseudorandom noise to pixel data before rounding, in order to diffuse quantization errors. The principle is that if each of a sequence of pixels is, say, about half way between two shades of gray, half the pixels should be pushed to the lighter shade and half to the darker shade. Similarly, intermediate colors may be obtained from a limited palette by using different colors in neighboring pixels, and counting on the eye to average them. The method provides a larger color space at the expense of lower effective resolution. In the case where only two shades are provided (such as a black on white laser printer), the method is sometimes called **digital halftoning.** Also, **dither** *v.t.* : to apply dithering; *adj.* : of or related to dither.

dither matrix : An array of numbers, used in adjacent blocks repeated over the screen, providing the pattern for dithering. The matrix number associated with the screen coordinates is added to the pixel value before rounding.

DOA *D-O-A*\ *adj.* : *D*ead *O*n *A*rrival; (a computer product) having a hardware fault that prevents operation when first received and set up.

domain *n.* : A group of computers on a network sharing the same data concerning interconnections and resources, and administered as a group.

dominant wavelength : The wavelength of monochromatic light that when mixed with white light visually matches a given color. The dominant wavelength need not necessarily be a component of the given color for the match to occur. —See METAMERIC MATCH.

doming \rhymes with *homing*\ *n.* : Outward deformation of the shadow mask of a color CRT due to heating by the electron beam. The deformation may cause errors in color purity; local doming is one factor limiting the maximum luminance in a region of a shadowmask display.

DORE *door-ray*\ : *D*ynamic *O*bject *R*endering *E*nvironment; a high- level graphics software interface originated by Ardent Computer Corp.

DOS *dahs*\ *D*isk *O*perating *S*ystem; *n.* 1 : The MS-DOS operating system developed by Microsoft, Inc., for IBM-compatible personal computers. 2 : Any disk operating system. Also, *adj.* : Compatible with the MS-DOS environment, particularly IBM-compatible personal computer hardware.

dot *n.* : A circular marker of adjustable size, used in graphics, especially for molecular modeling.

dot cloud : A set of dots, each typically one to two pixels in diameter, used in graphics for molecular modeling to represent certain transparent surfaces; in MCAD terminology, it is a type of polymarker.

double-buffer : In graphics, a partition of the frame buffer so that a new image can be constructed out of view in one buffer while a different image is being viewed in the other buffer, the roles of the buffers being continually interchanged for animation effects.

double hexcone : —See HEXCONE.

downloadable *adj.* : Capable of being sent from a host computer to an independent processing unit or peripheral device for local storage and subsequent quick access. For example, raster fonts *downloadable* into a printer for use by the printer when required.

DPCM : *D*ifferential *P*ulse *C*ode *M*odulation; a class of data-compression techniques that depend upon having an algorithm for predicting successive data from past data and encoding the differences between the predicted and actual data. To generate the differences, the prediction algorithm must be executed as part of the compression process. The prediction algorithm is run for de-compression, with the encoded differences added back to the predictions to reconstruct the quantized encoded value.

dpi [*alt*. DPI] : *d*ots *p*er *i*nch; the number of individually controllable printable marks per inch of paper for a printer using, typically, laser or ink-jet technology. The horizontal and vertical resolutions are generally assumed equal, unless explicitly specified otherwise.

dragging *n.* : Moving a graphics object under control of a pointing device. For example, repositioning a screen icon or a portion of a drawing using a mouse. Also, **drag** *v.t.* : to move by dragging.

DRAM *D-ram*\\ : *D*ynamic *R*andom *A*ccess *M*emory; a type of integrated circuit memory chip in which each bit is stored as a charge in a capacitor in the memory cell. This technique provides high storage density and correspondingly low cost, but it requires that data be accessed periodically to restore the charge in each cell. Restoration is usually done by setting aside dedicated *refresh cycles* under the control of special hardware.

Drawing Interchange Format : —See DIF.

DRC : *D*esign *R*ule *C*hecking; a software processing step used to validate silicon compiled layouts, hand layouts, and other chip designs to ensure that none of the designed layout violates the fabrication rules for spacing of elements and the like.

drum plotter : A pen plotter in which the paper (or other plotting media) is attached to a drum that rotates to accomplish one axis of positioning, while the pen holder is transported back and forth on a rail to provide the other axis of positioning.

DSP : *D*igital *S*ignal *P*rocessor; a computer oriented toward math-intensive applications, often a single chip or small chip set. Although named for application to digital signal processing, present devices are general-purpose and have a broad application in graphics and image processing.

DTP : —See DESKTOP PUBLISHING.

dual heads : A configuration of a single workstation processor with two monitors, generally operating so that a single cursor traverses both displays.

DVI : *D*igital *V*ideo *I*nteractive; technology for the compression and recon-struction of video imagery stored digitally, usually on optical disk.

DVMA : *D*evice *V*irtual *M*emory *A*ccess; virtual memory access initiated by a device in an I/O slot, as contrasted to access initiated by the CPU.

DVST : *Direct View Storage Tube;* a cathode ray tube designed to hold an image, usually written calligraphically, until erased in a separate operation.

DXP : Autodesk file format for graphics data.

Dynamic Object Rendering Environment : —See DORE.

dynamic random access memory : —See DRAM.

dynamic range *n.* 1 : The range of a signal or parameter from the smallest value to the largest value that can be represented or sensed by a system. For example, the dynamic range of human vision is about 10^{-5} ft.-lamberts to over 10^4 ft.-lamberts, from the threshold of dark-adapted vision to the brightest white objects in full sun. 2 : The ratio of the maximum intensity of a display to the minimum intensity, as measured in a dark environment and not necessarily within the same image. The dynamic range is typically much larger than the contrast that can be achieved within a single image viewed in an environment with ambient light.

E

E & S : —See EVANS AND SUTHERLAND, INC.

EBCDIC *ebcidick*\ : *E*xtended *B*inary *C*oded *D*ecimal *I*nterchange *C*ode; an IBM-originated eight-bit code for the representation of alphanumeric and control characters. The alternative *ASCII* code now predominates.

ECAD : *E*lectrical *C*omputer-*A*ided *D*esign; the market related to schematic capture, board layout, and IC design.

ECAE : *E*lectrical *C*omputer-*A*ided *E*ngineering; the application of computers to the analysis of electronic circuits and other electrical and electronic devices.

ECC : *E*rror *C*orrecting *C*ode[d]; mechanism [or property] of computer memory having additional stored bits and additional circuitry so as to correct one or more erroneous bits in retrieved data.

echo *v.t.* 1 : To provide a continuous display of the values being provided by a graphic input device, such as a dial box or digitizing tablet. 2 : More generally, to repeat any input data, such as keyboard input, to a display device.

ECL : *E*mitter-*C*oupled *L*ogic; family of electronic circuit components used for high-speed design characterized by multiple supply voltages, high power dissipation, and excellent transmission line drive capability.

edge merging : Filling the gaps resulting from cracking to permit a high-quality rendering of a surface.

EDIF : *E*lectronic *D*ata *I*nterchange *F*ormat; a standard format for exchanging CADDS data defined by *Electronic Design Interchange Format Version 2 : 0.0, EIA Interim Standard No. 44,* May 1987, ISBN 0-7908-000-4.

EEPROM *E-E-prom*\ : *E*lectrically *E*rasable *P*rogrammable *R*ead-Only *M*emory; a memory chip programmed electrically to hold data until erased electrically. Typically used to hold a small amount of configuration data when a system is powered down.

EGA : 1 [trademark, IBM Corp.] —See *E*nhanced *G*raphics *A*dapter. 2 : *E*nabling *G*raphics *A*ttribute; a binary variable controlling the presence or absence of a graphics attribute.

EIA : *E*lectronic *I*ndustries *A*ssociation.

44

EISA *ease-uh*\ : Extended Industry Standard Architecture; 32-bit bus interface standard for personal computer I/O adopted by industry consortium as an alternative to IBM's Micro-Channel interface.

electrical computer-aided design : —See ECAD.

electrical computer-aided engineering : —See ECAE.

electromagnetic deflection : Means of positioning the beam in a CRT using the magnetic field from external coils (the deflection yoke); commonly used for raster displays.

electronic imaging : The broad field encompassing image processing, including sensors for acquiring image data, storage, and retrieval systems and output devices.

electrophotographic printer : LASER PRINTER.

electrostatic deflection : Means of positioning the beam in a CRT using an electric field on deflection plates within the tube; commonly used in oscilloscopes and other applications where rapid beam positioning is required.

electrostatic plotter : A plotter comprising a row of adjacent tightly arrayed styli to deposit an image of electrical charges on the plotting media, which subsequently attracts a toner that is fused to the media by heat. Color plotting is accomplished either by rewinding the media for multiple passes with different-colored toners or by running the media through a series of similar devices having each dedicated to a color.

electrostatic printing : The technology related to forming an image by creating a pattern of electrical charge, using the charge to position toner on print media, and fusing the toner to the media to form a permanent image. This technology is used in various ways in electrostatic plotters, laser printers, copying machines, and other devices.

element *n.* : One of many small subdivisions of a space or object, created to facilitate the solution of a problem. For FINITE ELEMENT ANALYSIS, a solid object is conceptually subdivided into approximately cube-shaped elements whose physical properties are more easily modeled than the whole.

em *n.* : In typesetting, a unit of measure equal to the point size of the current font, and usually corresponding to the width of a capital "M." Usually applied to the width of a dash or space, as an **em dash** or **em space.**

emittance *n.* : Pertaining to light emitted by a surface.

emulation *n.* : —See SIMULATION.

en *n.* : In typesetting, a unit of measure equal to one-half an em. Usually applied to the width of a dash or space, as an **en dash** or **en space.**

encapsulated PostScript : A file of PostScript-compatible commands and data designed for transfer between application programs, or for inclusion in a document originating from multiple sources.

encoder *n.* 1 : Electronic device for converting separate red, green, and blue video signals into a single composite video signal for television. —See NTSC ENCODER. 2 : Software that converts the commands in a graphics language into a sequence of instructions compatible with a hardware interface to a graphics device.

end closure : CLOSURE.

end-effector *n.* : A gripper or other device at the end of a robotic manipulator.

Enhanced Graphics Adapter™ [IBM Corp.] : A standard interface and frame buffer specification for 350 x 640 pixel (up to) 16-color graphics for MS-DOS personal computers.

environment map : A means of aiding the rendering of reflecting surfaces of an object by first computing an image as a function of direction from the center point of the object, and then referencing the image according to the directions of reflected rays computed on the surface of the object. The map may be computed as projected on a cube.

EPLD *E-P-L-D*\\ : *E*lectrically *P*rogrammable *L*ogic *D*evice; any of a class of digital electronic components whose functionality can be altered by the user. Includes PROMs, PALs, GALs, logic cell arrays, and others.

EPROM *E-prom*\\ : *E*rasable *P*rogrammable *R*ead-*O*nly *M*emory; a memory chip programmed electrically to hold data until erased through a window on top of the chip package by exposure to intense ultraviolet light. Typically used to hold embedded programs or data in a system under development where changes are frequent, with cheaper ROM or PROM used in production.

EPS : The file extension used to designate mixed raster, text, and drawing files described by PostScript. —See ENCAPSULATED POSTSCRIPT.

equalizing pulses : Components of a video signal for an interlaced display that cause alternate fields to begin on full and half scanlines.

escape *n.* 1 : A means of providing device-dependent data through an otherwise device-independent software package, such as an implementation of a graphics standard. 2 : A means of providing control information in a data stream.

ESD : *E*lectrostatic *D*ischarge; source of integrated circuit chip damage in device handling caused by high input currents from static voltages built up by friction.

Ethernet *n.* : Widely used digital data network technology originated by Xerox Corp., using a single coaxial cable for communications.

Evans & Sutherland, Inc. : Utah-based supplier of graphics workstation equipment and flight simulation visual systems. One of the pioneering companies in computer graphics.

event *n.* : In the X Window System and, similarly, in other window systems, data generated asynchronously by a device or as a side effect of a client request that is received by a server and passed along to a client if the client previously asked to be informed.

execution thread : An instruction stream running on a single processor.

explicit surface : A parametric surface, for which each point on the surface is determined by evaluation of given parametric functions. —Compare IMPLICIT SURFACE.

extended light source : A source of illumination for graphics rendering, modeled such that light is emitted from a finite surface rather than just from a point; —See LIGHT SOURCE.

extension *n.* : —See FILE EXTENSION.

extent *n.* : The minimum and maximum coordinate values of a surface or other graphics object in each of the coordinate directions.

extent test : A test of whether or not a simple bounding surface, often a box, is clipped, in order to determine if graphics objects within are in view. —See CLIP TEST.

external alpha test : —See ALPHA TEST.

external (module) test : In JTAG scan-path testing, a mode whereby the diagnostic hardware is able to supply a stimulus to the output pins of one target module and sample the input pins of the module(s) that receive the output data; called *external* because the module-to-module interface can be tested independently of the module's functionality tests.

extraction *n.* : For an integrated circuit design, a software process that analyzes the geometric layout data to be used for mask making to derive the circuit network implied by the layout; the extracted network is then compared with the original design network as a check of the layout process.

extrude *v.t.* : To define a three-dimensional object by sweeping a two-dimensional shape over a three-dimensional curve. Generally, the plane of the two-dimensional shape is kept perpendicular to the curve. Also, **extrusion** *n*. : the resulting three-dimensional object.

Two-
dimensional
Shape

Three-
dimensional
Curve

Resulting Extrusion

eye point [*alt*. eyepoint] : —See VIEWPOINT.

eye-tracked display : A display system having a varying resolution and a means for sensing the eye and head position of the observer, so that graphics imagery of higher resolution is presented to the higher-resolution portion of the eye. Used mainly for flight simulation.

F

fab *n.* : *Fab*ricated; a bare printed circuit board, before components are installed.

face *n.* : A polygon that is part of a polyhedra or other graphics object.

face boundary : An edge of a polygon that maintains a logical association with the polygon when the edge is shared. Thus, a shared edge of a polyhedron comprises two face boundaries, one associated with each adjoining face.

face normal : A normalized vector specified for each polygon for the purpose of subsequent illumination calculations. The face normal is usually perpendicular to its associated polygon, but it may be altered to achieve a special illumination effect.

Face Normal

face sucker *n.* : Type of head mounted display using the rubber portion of a scuba mask to effect the light seal and attachment, especially an early product of this type produced by VPL Research, Inc.

facet *n.* : One of many flat surfaces, usually convex polygons, forming a surface.

faceting *n.* : The appearance that a surface is composed of polygons, especially when the objective was to shade it so as to appear smooth.

facsimile *adj.* : Related to equipment for digitally transmitting an image, including steps of digitally encoding the image, compressing the image data, transmitting the compressed data, and, on the receiving end : receiving, decompressing, and displaying the image. Also, *n.* : an image produced by facsimile transmission : fax.

fading : Simulation of the visual effects of atmospheric haze by mixing the color of a graphics object with a preselected **fading color** as a (usually exponentially weighted) function of the distance to the object. The fading color is usually white for day scenes and black for night scenes.

false coloring 1 : The reassignment of values in imagery obtained by sensors operating outside of the visible spectrum to visible colors for presentation, such as converting infrared data to shades of red for inclusion in an image. 2 : PSEUDOCOLORING. 3 : Producing intermediate colors by combining or dithering available primaries.

false contours : Apparent contours marking changes in color or intensity caused by quantization errors.

FAQ *fack*\\ : Frequently Asked Question; a file of common questions with their answers kept on a topical computer bulletin board to assist those new to the topic.

FARs \\rhymes with *cars*\\ : Federal Acquisition Requirements; the set of rules with which suppliers to the U.S. government must comply —many thousands of pages of them.

fast Fourier transform : An algorithm for efficiently computing the frequency components of a digitally sampled signal, used widely in digital signal processing. The basic algorithm, called the Cooley-Tukey algorithm, has spawned numerous variations.

fast Phong : A variation of *Phong shading* in which the Phong illumination model is evaluated at vertices, but an approximate nonlinear interpolation method is used within faces to speed the computations.

fat bits : A feature of a graphics paint system allowing a small portion of the image to be enlarged to the point where individual bits in the raster pattern are accessible for editing.

fault coverage : For an integrated circuit, the percentage of nodes that is toggled by the application of a set of test vectors designed to detect "stuck at" faults, i.e., nodes permanently a logic one or logic zero, 95 to 99 percent being considered good coverage.

fault coverage vectors : A set of binary test patterns for an integrated circuit designed to reveal a high percentage of the potential manufacturing flaws in the device. The **fault coverage** is the percentage of potential conditions in which an internal node is stuck, high or low, that the fault coverage vectors will detect.

fax [from facsimile] *adj.* : FACSIMILE. Also, *v.t.* : to send by fax machine; *n.* : an image sent by fax machine.

FBI *F-B-I*\\ : Finished Board Inventory; completed electronic circuit boards awaiting installation or shipment.

FCC *F-C-C*\\ : Federal Communications Commission; the U.S. government agency responsible for the certification of electronic equipment for compliance with standards for spurious emissions potentially causing radio interference.

FCS *F-C-S*\\ : First Customer Shipment; the date on which a product is first shipped to a regular paying customer.

FDDI *F-D-D-I*\\ : *Fiber Distributed Data Interface*; interface to a high-bandwidth fiber-optic digital data network.

FEA : *Finite Element Analysis*; the analytical techniques applied to finite element models. —See FINITE ELEMENT MODELING.

Federal Acquisition Requirements : —See FARs.

Federal Communications Commission : —See FCC.

FEM : —See FINITE ELEMENT MODELING.

Feshner's law : That the perceived response to a sensory stimulus is proportional to the logarithm of the intensity of the stimulus. This leads to logarithmically derived measures for luminosity. While the logarithmic model is reasonable, a cube-root proportionality is now favored and is used for CIELW and CIELAB color spaces.

FFT *F-F-T*\\ : —See FAST FOURIER TRANSFORM.

Fiber Distributed Data Interface : —See FDDI.

field *n.* : In video for a scanned display, the data contained within a single traversal of the screen. For television video, a field corresponds to the data displayed on either the even or odd numbered scanlines, which are shown in a single vertical scan of the CRT display, and two fields, making a frame, are required to display the complete image. Also, *adj.* : related to a field. —See also FRAME, INTERLACE.

field frequency : The number of displayed video fields per second.

field-of-view : The angle in space covered by a display relative to an assumed eye point position. In some displays for flight simulation, different portions of the display can be seen from different eye point positions. For such displays, the *instantaneous* field-of-view is that from a single nominal eye point position, and the *total* field-of-view is the composite seen from all positions. —See WAC WINDOW.

field rendering : Rendering only the scanlines that will appear in one field of an interlaced video image.

field replaceable unit : —See FRU.

field-sequential *adj.* : Pertaining to a color display in which separately colored images are presented rapidly in sequence.

FIFO *figh-foe*\\ : *First-In First-Out*; a digital electronic memory circuit organized with two ports, one for entering data and one for removing data. The circuit queues data between the ports (up to specified depth) so that the first data entered is the first removed. The analogous technique applied in software is a *circular buffer*.

file extension : The portion of a computer file name appearing after the separator dot, or after the leftmost nonleading dot if there is more than one. For example, if a file is called "NAME.XYZ," then "XYZ" is the extension. By convention, the extension is often used to indicate the type of file or its format. Most commonly, the extension is abbreviated to either one or three letters.

file server : A computer on a network providing shared storage for programs and data.

fill *v.t.* : To render the interior of a graphics object, especially by changing the colors of pixels within a defined boundary. Also, *adj.* : related to fill, as *fill color* or *fill pattern*.

filled *adj.* : With respect to a polygon or other graphics object, rendered with a color, shade, or pattern over the surface, as opposed to being rendered with only the perimeter of the surface represented. —Compare HOLLOW-FILLED.

fillet *n.* : BLEND SURFACE.

film recorder : A device for outputting digital images to film, especially, high-resolution imagery to motion picture film for commercial animation.

filter *n.* 1 : A means of altering a signal by changing its component frequencies. An electronic circuit may accomplish this directly on a signal, for example, by attenuating unwanted high-frequency components. A **digital filter** is applied, typically, with software, and is used, for example, to enhance the high spatial frequencies corresponding to edges in an image. 2 : A computer program having, usually, a single data file as input and producing a single data file as output, performing a function such as data editing or reformatting.

filter function : A convolution kernel for antialiasing.

finished board inventory : —See FBI.

finite element modeling : Logical subdivision of a mechanical structure into small, often cubelike, pieces so that engineering computations are facilitated. For example, the stress analysis of a machine part under load may be computed by the interaction of forces on the elements of a model of the part; results are often presented by pseudocoloring a graphics image.

firmware [prob. *firm,* difficult to alter + *ware,* product] *n.* : Originally, the permanent code included in ROM for a microcoded processor. Now used for any vendor-supplied embedded software needed for use by a processor to carry out higher-level functions, such as the graphics code embedded in a graphics accelerator. The code is usually downloaded to a RAM and transparent to the user.

first customer shipment : —See FCS.

first-in first-out memory : —See FIFO.

fixing *n.* : FUSING.

flatbed plotter : A pen plotter working on a flat surface over which moves a carriage with a sliding pen holder.

flat shading : Means of computing the illumination effects on a graphics object made of polygons in which one value is computed and applied to each polygon, typically producing a faceted appearance; uniform shading.

flat square tube : —See FST.

flatten *v.t.* : To convert a hierarchical data structure into a nonhierarchical one, usually by applying inclusion criteria at the nodes of the hierarchy; typically, a user will flatten an application database structure to build a display list for rendering.

flattened display list : A display list having, at most, one level of hierarchy.

flicker *n.* : A defect of video imagery caused by too low a refresh rate, in which the image appears to flash or strobe.

flight simulation graphics : The application area of graphics technology dealing with the preparation of imagery for real-time interaction with a pilot under training in a flight simulator. The flight simulator provides controls, cockpit instrumentation, and, often, computer-controlled motion cues, while the graphics system provides imagery consistent with the control motions and other elements of the simulation. Training involving potentially hazardous situations, costly equipment, or difficult-to-control circumstances (such as rarely encountered weather phenomena) justifies the high cost of flight simulation graphics systems producing complex imagery. Other types of vehicle simulation graphics are categorized under the general heading of *flight simulation,* even if flight is not involved.

flood filling : Changing the interior color or pattern of a two-dimensional graphics object having a defined boundary by starting at an arbitrary interior point and changing pixels adjacent to those already filled until the entire interior is covered.

FLT : The MultiGen FLIGHT format for simulation databases.

flying spot scanner : A device for converting a film image to video by illuminating the film with a raster scanned spot of constant intensity, often produced by a CRT, and detecting the amount of light transmitted through the image as a function of time.

Foley and van Dam : Popular computer graphics text by James D. Foley and Andries van Dam, et. al. (1990). *Computer Graphics Principles and Practice*, 2nd ed., Reading, MA: Addison-Wesley Publishing Co.

folio *n.* : In typesetting, the page number or page number position in the layout of a page. Also, *v.t.* : to number pages consecutively.

font *n.* 1 : A family of letterforms sharing a particular style, but typically having character sets for normal, boldface, and italic versions in varying sizes. For example, the Helvetica font. : TYPEFACE. 2 : More traditionally, a letterform for a single particular size and style. For example, the 12-point Helvetica bold font. 3 : In a window system or graphics application, an array of glyphs supplied for use by a client.

footcandle *n.* : A unit of illuminance, i.e., light incident on a surface per unit area, equal to 10.76 lux. The footcandle was the traditional engineering unit of illuminance, but international standards now favor use of the *lux*.

footlambert *n.* : A unit of luminance, i.e., photometric brightness of a surface, equal to 3.426 nits. The footlambert was the traditional engineering unit of brightness, but international standards now favor use of the *nit*.

force display *n.* : Any device that communicates forces to a user.

force feedback *n.* : External forces applied to a user by an electronic system as a means of communicating information. —See TACTILE FEEDBACK.

forward differencing : An efficient means of evaluating a bicubic function iteratively to obtain a set of points on a surface. The *forward difference* of a function is the amount the function changes when its argument is incremented by a finite step. For bicubic functions, forward difference calculations reduce to a small set of multiplications and additions that may be repeated to obtain points on the surface.

4 : 2 : 2 *four-two-two*\ : The encoding of the information in a pixel, especially for digital video, in which four bits are allocated to luminance and two bits each to the I and Q color components.

FOV : —See FIELD-OF-VIEW.

foveal vision : The region of high-resolution vision near the center of view in the eye, used to look at an object. The total resolution of the human eye is less than 512 x 512 pixels, distributed nonlinearly. The illusion of uniformly high-resolution vision is caused by moving the foveal region throughout a scene.

FPA : Floating Point Accelerator; specialized hardware added to a computer system, often as an option, to increase the speed of floating point arithmetic.

fractal [coined by Benoit Mandelbrot from Latin *fractus,* broken. c. 1977] *n.* : A mathematical function, usually having a geometric interpretation, containing elements of self-similarity. The self-similarity may be identical, in which a portion of the function (or image) exactly replicates the whole on a different scale, or the self-similarity may be statistical, in which average or other statistical properties are reproduced on a different scale. Natural phenomena such as cloud and terrain forms are fractals having statistical self-similarity; the gross size of a portion of these structures cannot be estimated from scaleless images. Also, *adj.* : having the characteristics of a fractal.

frame *n.* : A single complete video image. For interlaced video, the frame consists of two fields containing, successively, the odd and even numbered raster lines of the image. For a noninterlaced image, a single field contains the entire frame.

frame buffer 1 : A hardware device having a computer interface for receiving input, a memory organized with data for each pixel, and circuitry for generating video output signals suitable for displaying all or part of the stored data as an image. The frame buffer is typically a circuit board plugged into a computer assembly. 2 : The memory associated with the color or intensity components, only, of a pixel image. 3 : The memory associated with the pixels of a stored image including displayable color and intensity data, and additional data not necessarily displayed. The additional data may include a z-buffer, window ID planes, overlay planes, cursor planes, or an alpha channel.

frame buffer port : In a graphics accelerator, the hardware interface that bypasses the accelerator to permit direct writing to the frame buffer : —See also DIRECT PORT : HOST PORT.

frame grabber : A device for capturing a frame of video imagery by converting it to a sequence of digital samples and storing the samples as pixels for access by a computer.

free-form *adj* : Drawn or sculpted freehand, without regard to precisely describing mathematical or geometrical forms. Such forms are modeled in computer graphics by a set of adjoining curve segments or curved-surface patches.

free-form surface *n.* : a surface defined with general curved surfaces, rather than being restricted to a polygonal or other more restrictive elements.

Fresnel equation : An equation giving the attenuation of a reflected beam of unpolarized light as a function of the angle of incidence, the wavelength, and the constant properties of the material. Used in ray tracing.

fringing *n.* : COLOR EDGING.

frisket *n.* : In publishing, an area of artwork protected from airbrushing, and by analogy, a portion of an image in a graphics or imaging system that is protected from modification.

front clipping plane : The HITHER plane.

front end : In a graphics accelerator, the portion of the system that receives data from the host computer and processes the coordinate conversions, illumination calculations, and other primitive-level tasks, in preparation for pixel-by-pixel rendering.

FRU : *F*ield *R*eplaceable *U*nit; a component, module, or assembly designed to be replaced as a unit when a failure within it is found at a customer site; it is a matter of policy as to what is deemed repairable at a customer site, but it is nowadays rare to make site repairs below the circuit board level.

frustum of vision : The three-dimensional space within which graphics objects are viewed. The space is enclosed by top, bottom, left, and right planes, all passing though the viewpoint, plus near and far clipping planes meant to exclude obscuring and uninteresting data, respectively.

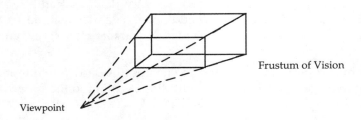

Frustum of Vision

Viewpoint

FST : *F*lat *S*quare *T*ube; a cathode ray tube having a cylindrical front surface (well, it is flatter than a spherical front surface) and rather square corners (the front surface is conventionally rectangular in aspect).

FTG Data Systems : Stanton, CA, vendor of light pens.

function keys : Separate keys on a computer keyboard, usually labeled with a letter and a sequence number (such as F1 through F10), that are left for use by applications programs.

fusing *n.* : In electrostatic printing technology, the process of permanently adhering toner particles to the print media, typically through the application of heat or pressure : FIXING.

Futurebus+ *n.* : A standard (IEEE 896.3) computer bus architecture designed for scalable performance in single- or multiprocessing computer systems. Primarily 64 bits, but having extensions upwards and downwards. The standard supports a dual-bus concept in which VME, EISA, or another bus is used for I/O with Futurebus+ for processors and memory.

fuzzy rug : Scientific visualization technique producing a height-field display from a gray-scaled image, wherein height is proportional to gray scale intensity; used for finding coherent signals in noise. Called a *waterfall display* when new data are added at the top as old data fall off the bottom.

G

GaAs \ *gas*\ *n.* : *G*allium *A*rsenide; material having a higher electron mobility than silicon and, therefore, offering potentially greater circuit operating speeds—at the expense of material processing difficulty.

GAL : *G*eneric *A*rray *L*ogic; a type of programmable logic device originated by Lattice Semiconductor, Inc.

gamma correction : Means for compensating for the typical nonlinear response of a CRT display, often with a table look-up. The intensity displayed by a CRT is proportional to the applied voltage raised to the gamma power, where gamma is typically in the range 2.3 to 2.8. Failure to apply a compensating correction results in images that lack contrast. Television signals are gamma corrected to a standard value before transmission.

gamut *n.* : The range of colors that can be produced by a display or output device. The full gamut includes luminance and may be represented as a three-dimensional volume in CIE XYZ color space. The chromaticity portion of the gamut may be represented on a chromaticity diagram; for example, the gamut of a color monitor may be plotted as a triangular region on a CIE color space diagram, with the phosphor colors as the vertices of the triangle. A color that cannot be produced by a particular device is **out-of-gamut** for that device.

gamut mapping : Transforming color data from that designed for an output device having a particular gamut to that suited to a different device and gamut.

Gantt chart : A bar graph showing planned activities as a function of time, usually sorted in order of planned start time with one activity per line.

gas plasma display : A plasma display.

gate array : A type of integrated circuit in which diffused silicon wafers having a standard pattern of gates or transistors are adapted to particular designs by customized layers of metal interconnections added to the standard wafers.

gateway *n.* : A hardware device that permits exchange of data between two networks.

gaze direction : The direction of view.

58

GEM 1 : The file extension designating bit-mapped image formatted files compatible with the personal computer paint program *GEM Paint*. 2 : The file extension designating object-oriented formatted files compatible with the personal computer drawing program *GEM Artline*.

generalized polygon : —See POLYGON, GENERALIZED.

genlock [prob. from *sync generator locking*] *n.* : The capability of a video device to accept a synchronization signal so that the input or output pixels of the device are precisely in phase with the synchronization signal. Also, *v.t.* : To accept video synchronization.

geographic information system : —See GIS.

geometric object : A two- or three-dimensional shape.

geometric primitive : One of a set of mathematically defined shapes specified for rendering by a graphics system. Typically includes points, lines, and triangles, and may extend to polyhedra and curved surfaces. All input geometric data for a graphics system must be specified as combinations of the geometric primitives defined for the system. —See GRAPHICS OBJECT.

geometry *n.* 1 : Adjective applied to graphics operations at the level of vertices, edges, and polygons, such as transformation and clipping, as opposed to rendering. 2 : Sometimes used to mean *graphics,* with *graphics* being redefined to include image processing.

Geometry Engine : An ASIC designed for early Silicon Graphics, Inc., products having selectable microcode on-chip. The front end of the accelerator was formed by Geometry Engines in series, each performing selected operations in the transformation pipeline.

geospecific texture [mainly flight simulation] : Texture derived from aerial or satellite photographs mapped onto the corresponding graphic model of real terrain.

ghosting *n.* 1 : In electrostatic printing, the unintended transfer of portions of one image to a successor image, usually due to the presence of residual toner. 2 : In video and, especially, television technology, the appearance of an unintended offset secondary image in a display due to a delayed reflection of the video signal. Also, **ghost** *n.* : the secondary image present in ghosting.

GIF : *G*raphics *I*nterchange *F*ormat; a file format developed by CompuServe for color image data.

gigabyte *n.* 1 : 2^{30} bytes, 1024 megabytes. 2 : 1000 megabytes.

gigaflop *n.* : A billion floating point operations.

GIS : *G*eographic *I*nformation *S*ystem; a system for the organized storage, retrieval, and manipulation of maps and other geographic data.

GKS : *G*raphical *K*ernel *S*ystem; a graphics-software standard, originally oriented toward two-dimensional applications. Specified by ANSI X3.124-1985.

GKS metafile : A file format understood by GKS using, in one version, ASCII characters for machine independence.

gloss *n.* : The visual effect of a blurred specular highlight, as from a waxed surface.

glyph n. : One of a stored set of bit-mapped images representing the characters or other symbols comprising a font. Also, **interglyph** *adj.* : between glyphs, as interglyph spacing.

golden board : A printed circuit board or assembly that is stipulated to be a defect-free example of the embodied design, and that may, therefore, be used as a reference for extracting test data.

Gouraud shading *goo-rho*\ [originated by Tlenri Gouraud, 1971] : Smooth variation of surface intensity over a triangle or quadrilateral computed by bilinearly interpolating the intensities from the vertices. More complex polygons and polyhedra may be shaded by decomposing them into triangular or quadrilateral regions.

GPCI *gypsy*\ : *G*raphics *P*rocessor *C*ommand *I*nterface; Sun Microsystems programming library for the GP family of graphics accelerators. Closely tied to the hardware interface.

grab *v.t.* : In a window system environment, to take control by a client, for exclusive use, of an input device, server, or other system device or resource.

graftal *n.* : A class of graphics objects sharing some of the properties of fractals in which the rules for generation permit local modification of properties. Notably applied to the generation of images of plant life.

granularity *n.* : the relative fidelity of a simulation, esp. as related to the amount of detail included to make the simulation realistic; a fine-grained simulation has more details included than a coarse-grained simulation.

Graphical Kernel System : —See GKS.

graphics *n.* 1 : Computer graphics. 2 [uncommon] : Graphics plus image processing and video : VISUAL COMPUTING.

Graphics Interchange Format : —See GIF.

graphics object : One or more geometric primitives usually corresponding to an element of a scene to be rendered, grouped as an *object* for convenience in managing the database.

graphics pipeline : The ordered sequence of operations performed on primitives as they are processed by a graphics system. The sequence may, for example, comprise a number of geometric transformations with clipping operations defined and applied in the different coordinate systems current at different points in the pipeline. Definition of the graphics pipeline is closely tied to the variety of operations and parameters available to the system user.

graphics primitive : —See PRIMITIVE.

graphics terminal 1 : A graphics device driven as a peripheral by a separate host computer. The graphics terminal contains memory for a display list in a format specific to the hardware, and it computes and displays the imagery from the single locally stored list. 2 : The style of graphics accelerator system on a workstation in which the graphics resources of the accelerator are not shared or minimally shared among concurrent applications. For example, the window system may run with a separate frame buffer having a hole cut by logic to reveal the frame buffer of the accelerated application.

gravity *n.* 1 : In two-dimensional graphics, especially drawing applications, the use of an implied region around a preexisting graphics object, such that when a vertex for a new object is created within the gravity region, the vertex will be placed at the nearest point on the preexisting object. 2 : In the X Window System, the set of rules determining how the elements in a window will be rearranged when the window size is changed.

gray scale [*less commonly* grayscale] *n.* 1 : The number of shades of gray a display system in a particular viewing environment can produce, usually with steps of the square root of two in intensity between successive shades. Since steps of the square root of two are generally clearly perceptible, the implied emphasis is on having shades of gray that are distinct, as opposed to the concern for continuous-tone imagery of having enough steps so that changes will not be perceived as steps. 2 : A strip of adjacent equal-sized regions filled with progressing shades of gray, usually included in an image for quality control or calibration purposes. Also, *adj.* : Having more than two shades of gray.

greeking *n.* : The use of bars or boxes instead of text in a representation of a page layout.

greek text : In publishing, generic text used in lieu of final copy to facilitate the layout of a page. The traditional text is actually Latin.

grid *n.* 1 [*alt.* grid alignment] : A reference cross-hatch, either displayed or implied, in a drawing package so that newly created vertices are placed at the nearest cross-hatch intersection. The objective is to simplify the alignment of elements in the drawing. 2 : Reference lines included in a graph or chart to help in determining the numerical values of the data. 3 : A graphics object comprising horizontal and vertical lines of specified numbers and spacing, as generated by a drawing or paint program for inclusion in a user's work.

grip *n.* : The area near the edges of a printed page that cannot receive print because the space is reserved for the printing mechanism to hold the paper. A region of 1/2 inch on each edge is common for laser printers.

grit wheel plotter : A type of pen plotter in which paper is spooled back and forth around a drum. The edges of the paper are embossed with a pattern by wheels on the drum ends having a sandpaperlike surface that ensure accurate reregistration of the paper as it is spooled.

ground mapping : —See MAP.

guard-band clipping : A technique for clipping three-dimensional data, in which the three-dimensional clipping limits corresponding to the perimeter of the clip region are enlarged, with data subsequently rendered in the enlarged regions subsequently removed by two-dimensional clipping. The motivation for the technique is to increase rendering throughput by greater use of efficient two-dimensional clipping instead of computationally difficult three-dimensional clipping. Savings can sometimes be achieved in spite of the cost of generating some out-of-view pixels.

GUI *gooey**n.:* Graphical *User* *Interface;* A computer-to-human interface that features graphics elements for input and output of data, most typically the windows, icons, menus, and pointing device [WIMP] style.

gull wing *adj.* : Pertaining to a type of integrated circuit package for surface mounting, in which flat leads emerging radially from the package are bent down to the level of the bottom of the body of the package.

Gull Wing Component on Circuit Board

Gupta-Sproull algorithm : A means of drawing antialiased lines assuming a conical *convolution kernel* having a diameter of two pixels. The algorithm exploits the Bresenham line drawing scheme, and it always paints three-pixel-wide lines. It is relatively simple to implement, only requiring the determination of the perpendicular distance from the pixel center to the line center, and a table look-up based on this distance, to determine the appropriate filter value to use.

gutter *n.* 1 : In publishing, the inside margins between the facing pages of text in a document. 2 : The extra space added to the normal inside margins of the pages of a document to allow for binding. 3 [less common] : The space between columns on a page.

H

halation *n*. : Reflections within the glass face plate of a CRT that limit the contrast of neighboring pixels.

half-toning [*alt*. halftoning] *n*. : The use of *dithering* with only black and white to approximate continuous-tone imagery. In conventional printing, the use of a photographic screen technique whereby continuous tones are approximated by printing an array of dots of varying sizes so that larger dots correspond to the darker image tones. Also, **half-tone** *v.t.* : To apply half-toning.

haloed line : A line drawn continuous, while lines intersecting it are drawn with gaps around the potential points of intersection.

handle *n*. : One of a group of symbols, such as a small filled square, associated with a graphics object as displayed by a drawing package. Selecting and dragging one of the handles changes the scale of the object in one or both dimensions.

haptic *adj*. : Related to the sense of touch.

hard copy [*alt*. hardcopy] *n*. 1 : Computer output printed on paper, as opposed to *soft copy* reproduced on diskette or other media. 2 : In publishing, a manuscript to be typeset. 3 [uncommon] : Card stock rather than paper.

hard return : In word processing, a carriage return entered by the user and kept as part of the input text. —Compare SOFT RETURN.

hardware : Electronic circuitry; physical elements above the level of circuit components, including board stiffeners, board edge connectors, fans, chassis, and case, are sometimes referred to as *mechanical*.

hardware pan and zoom : —See PAN, ZOOM.

HDTV : *H*igh-*D*efinition *Tele*V*ision*; as yet nonstandardized format for high-resolution television, generally featuring about 1100 scanlines in a 3:5 aspect ratio format.

head gear *n*. : Apparatus worn on the head to facilitate virtual reality; usually including a head mounted display, a tracker, and a stereo headset.

head-mounted display : —See HELMET MOUNTED DISPLAY.

head tracking : Determining the position of an observer's head by various electronic, mechanical, optical, or acoustic techniques, so that graphics imagery may be computed corresponding to changes from a nominal viewpoint. Used for specialized applications, notably, simulation and military aircraft helmet-mounted displays. Also, **head-tracked** *adj.* : Having the graphics image computed according to a position and direction derived from head tracking. —See also HELMET-MOUNTED DISPLAY, POLHEMUS CORP., VIRTUAL REALITY.

head-up display : —See HUD.

hedgehog *n.* : A display of a three-dimensional object as a wireframe with associated normal vectors.

helmet-mounted display [*alt.* head-mounted display] *n.* 1 : A display device in which the display is attached to a head-tracked helmet worn by the user. For visual simulation, the image may be transferred by fiber optics to an optical assembly on the helmet, or a small CRT or LCD display is attached directly to the helmet; stereo viewing is typically provided through the use of a display for each eye. For military applications, imagery is projected to the inside of a faceplate or to a beamsplitter over one eye, so that graphics imagery is superimposed on the view of the real world. 2 : A head-mounted display.

hemi-cube *n.* : A mapping of the directions in a hemisphere to the surface of a cube, similar to the mapping of a sphere to a *direction cube*.

Hershey fonts : A set of stroke letterforms originated in the U.S. Bureau of Standards and placed in the public domain.

heterogeneous *adj.* : Composed of elements of different types, such as a heterogeneous computing environment having computers from different manufacturers or of differing capabilities.

heterogeneous network : A network serving computers having different architectures.

Hewlett-Packard Graphics Language : —See HPGL.

Hewlett-Packard, Inc. : Cupertino, CA, company; a major supplier of computers, workstations, graphics, and peripheral equipment.

hexadecimal [*abbrev* hex] *n.* : The base-16 number system, convenient for computer systems because four-bit patterns [0000, .. ., 0101, 0110, ... , 1111] each correspond to a single hexadecimal symbol [0, ..., 9, A, ..., F]. Also, *adj.* : being in base 16.

hexcone color solid [originated by Alvy Ray Smith, 1978] : A color space defined by red, yellow, green, cyan, blue, and magenta on the vertices of a hexagon, white at the center of the hexagon, and having black at a point below the center of the hexagon. Also called the **HSV hexcone**. The **double hexcone** model is similar, with white at a point symmetric to black above the center of the hexagon.

hidden line removal : A process yielding a wireframe rendering in which lines are removed corresponding to the edges that would have been occluded in a rendering of surfaces. The net effect is as if surfaces were rendered in the background color.

Hidden Line Removal

Before   After

hidden surface algorithm : Any algorithm that solves the *hidden surface problem*, or closely approximates a solution.

hidden surface problem : The fundamental problem of determining which portions of modeled three-dimensional objects should be visible in a rendered graphics scene and which portions are occluded by intervening objects.

hidden surface removal : The process of applying a hidden surface algorithm to solve the hidden surface problem.

high-definition television : —See HDTV.

highlight *n.* 1 : A bright region of an image of a shiny object, usually corresponding to the specular reflection of a light source. 2 : The brightest value in a continuous-tone image.

highlighting *n.* : Altering the appearance of a graphics object, by making it brighter or by other means, to identify it. Also, **highlight** *v.t.* : To apply highlighting.

high resolution : With respect to a display or output imaging device, having a large number of pixels per scanline and large number of scanlines. The actual numbers depend upon the state of technology and the particular application. For personal computer color displays, 800 x 600 or 1024 x 768 may presently qualify. For workstations, 1280 x 1024 or 1600 x 1280 are typically high resolution. For slide-making, motion-picture animation, and certain publishing applications, resolutions from 2000 x 2000 to 4000 x 4000 may be implied by high resolution.

HIL : *H*uman *I*nterface *L*oop; Hewlett-Packard–originated interface bus for graphics input devices and the like.

hiragana *n.* : The set of about 100 curvilinear characters used in Japanese mainly to affix verb endings and the like to basic kanji. —Compare KATAKANA.

histogram equalization : In image processing, a means of adjusting the contrast characteristics of an image to provide more visible detail. The intensity values of the pixels of an image are first counted in subranges of intensity, forming histogram data. Tables are then constructed to reassign intensity values so that the data will cover the range of visible shades of intensity, and image subsequently transformed accordingly. Thus, for example, if the original image data are clustered in a narrow range near a single intensity level, the processed image will cover the full range and have a much more apparent detail.

hither *n.* 1 : A clipping plane perpendicular to the line-of-sight serving to exclude data too close to the viewpoint and behind it; the forward clipping plane. 2 : The distance along the line of sight from the viewpoint to the forward clipping plane. Also, *adj.* : related to hither.

HIT Lab : The *H*uman *I*nterface *T*echnology *Lab*oratory, University of Washington, Seattle, WA 98195.

hollow fill : Rendering of a graphics database in which only the pixels adjacent to a polygon edge are displayed, while maintaining all properties of color, illumination, and depth cueing. The rules for exactly which pixels are touched on the edge are those for polygons rather than the possibly different rules for vectors. —Compare WIREFRAME.

Holodeck [from the science fiction television series "Star Trek: The Next Generation"; presumably from *holo* holographic + *deck* ship's deck] *n.*: a fictional device for generating virtual environments in which the users are not encumbered by apparatus and in which the experience appears real in every aspect.

homogeneous coordinates : A generalization of Euclidean space in which an additional dimension, the homogeneous coordinate, is added. For example, for three-dimensional graphics, a 4 x 4 transformation matrix is used. Using homogenous coordinates, translation and rotation information can be kept in a single matrix for convenience in applying successive coordinate transformations.

homogeneous network : A computer network serving only computers of the same architecture.

host *n.* : In a multiprocessor system, a processor that manages requests for resources or services from other processors. Typically, the concept is used when specialized processors such as graphics accelerators work with a general-purpose processor that is running an operating system or control program.

host port : —See DIRECT PORT.

hot-spot [*alt.* hotspot] *n.* 1 : A point associated with the rendered image of a graphics object used for positioning, clipping, or other purposes. 2 : In the X Window System, the point associated with the cursor.

hot-spot clipping : A simple means of clipping in which a single point on the graphics object is tested for proximity to the scene boundary, and the entire object is eliminated if the point is too close to a boundary.

HPGL : *H*ewlett-*P*ackard *G*raphics *L*anguage; interface format originated for driving Hewlett-Packard plotters, now used more widely as an object-oriented drawing format.

HSL : *H*ue, *S*aturation, and *L*ightness; means of specifying a color alternative to using the red, green, and blue components.

HSL cylinder [originated by Joblove and Greenberg, 1978] : A representation of perceptual color space as a cylindrical solid having white on the top surface, black on the bottom surface, and saturated colors around the circumference of the middle cross section.

HSV : *H*ue, *S*aturation, and *V*alue; means of specifying a color alternative to using the red, green, and blue components.

HSV hexcone : —See HEXCONE.

HUD *hud*\ : *H*ead-*U*p *D*isplay; a display system in which a vehicle operator views symbology superimposed on an out-the-window view of the world. Developed for military aviation, the technology has been applied to commercial aviation and automobiles.

hue *n.* : The property of a color that distinguishes the colors of the spectrum from each other.

Huffman coding : An efficient means of compressing a binary data stream by assigning variable-length codes to bit patterns based upon the statistics of how often various patterns occur. The shortest codes are assigned to the most frequently appearing patterns.

hull *n.* : A graphics construct that encloses another construct or collection of constructs having the same number of dimensions; the hull usually has a simpler form than that which is enclosed.

Human Interface Loop : —See HIL.

HW : —See HARDWARE.

HyperCard *n.* : A program for accessing data, originated by Apple Computer, in which data are presented in text and graphics fields on a graphics image called a *card*. The fields may be accessed individually to yield additional cards of data and references. The collection of cards is called a *stack*.

hypermedia *n.* : Extension of hypertext to access animated sequences and sound as well as text and static images.

hypertext [coined by Ted Nelson, c. 1965] *n.* : Accessing of information by selecting a portion of a figure or text as a means of calling up additional data, which, in general, may be similarly referenced. Data are generally cross-linked to allow access that is not strictly hierarchical.

I

I *n.* : The in-phase component of an encoded color video signal, or the corresponding orange-to-cyan component of a color coordinate space. —See YIQ SPACE.

IBM : *I*nternational *B*usiness *M*achines; as you may have heard, the world's largest computer company; a late entrant in the graphics workstation aspect of the business, however.

ICE : *I*n-*C*ircuit *E*mulator; a hardware device that plugs into the socket, usually holding a processor chip for the purpose of obtaining special capabilities for debugging of the software and hardware associated with the processor in its application.

icon *n.* : A graphics symbol, as opposed to alphabetic name, representing a computer program or program function used so that the program or function may be initiated by selecting the icon.

iconify *v.t.* : To suspend a program or close and remove the window through which the user interacted with the program, and to subsequently represent the program by an icon. To **de-iconify** is to reopen the window and resume the operation, in doing so, also eliminating the icon while the program is executing.

IEEE *I-triple E*\: *I*nstitute of *E*lectrical and *E*lectronic *E*ngineers; professional society headquartered in New York with international membership; publishes a wide variety of professional journals and magazines and establishes industry standards for aspects of computers and electronics.

IGES *eyejess*\ : *I*nitial *G*raphics *E*xchange *S*pecification; a standard file format for graphics data interchange, particularly applied to mechanical CAD databases, published by the U.S. National Institute of Standards and Technology (formerly, National Bureau of Standards).

illuminance *n.* 1 : The flux density striking an illuminated surface. Measured in lumens per square meter (which equals lux). 2 : A programming construct in RenderMan that facilitates collection of the light source contributions to a surface from within a specified angle of a specified direction.

illuminant *n.* : A light source having a specified color spectrum, such as one of the several CIE illuminants. Specification of an illuminant is important for critical comparison of reflective color samples, as the appearance of inks and dyes will change with the spectrum of the light source used for viewing.

illumination *n.* : All of the calculations related to the presence of light sources performed in the preparation of a graphics image.

image *n.* : An array of pixels containing information for viewing; an image may be from computer graphics, image processing, a digitized input, or other means.

image analysis : The branch of image processing dealing with identifying features in an image, grouping the features into objects, and classifying the objects, all as steps toward providing a useful understanding of the image content.

image composition *n.* : Rendering a graphics image by separately computing two or more partial images and subsequently combining them into one image. The combining process may use a predetermined occlusion order or each pixel may have an associated distance used to perform occlusion on a pixel-by-pixel basis.

image definition area : The space, typically larger than the viewport or screen, over which an image may be viewed by panning and zooming within the application.

image processing : The class of processing operations for which the input is a pixel image. The output is typically also a pixel image, but may comprise feature or other data derived from the image. The distinction from computer graphics is that computer graphics starts with a modeled database from which an image is produced, whereas image processing starts with an image to produce another image (or data).

IMG : A file extension designating bit-mapped image files produced as an alternate format by personal computer paint programs *GEM Paint* and *Halo DPE*.

immediate mode 1 : Type of graphics interface in which each object is rendered upon being given to the graphics system, as opposed to initiating rendering by a separate command that references a predefined list of objects. 2 : [less commonly] A style of graphics programming in which the user does not keep a list of the graphics sent to the graphics system, so that, for example, there is no list that could be later retraversed for rerendering.

immersive virtual reality *n.* : an electronic simulation in which perspective images are generated in real time from a stored database corresponding to the position and orientation of the head of a user, who observes the images on a head mounted display, and in which three-dimensional sound cues are provided as well as a means for interacting with objects in the database.

implicit surface : A surface defined as the locus of points satisfying a given set of equations. For example, the points on a unit sphere are defined implicitly as the [x,y,z] values satisfying the equation $x^2 + y^2 + z^2 = 1$. —Compare EXPLICIT SURFACE.

inbetween *n.* : A frame produced by inbetweening. pl. **inbetweens.**

inbetweening *n.* : The computation of intermediate graphics objects that approximates steps in the transitions from a given initial form to a given final form. Sometimes used for generating intermediate frames in animated sequences.

independent software vendor : —See ISV.

indexed color : A way of storing and manipulating color information in a graphics system by associating an integer number with the graphics element, and using that number to subsequently look up a description of the color in a table; color changes may thus be made by only altering the look-up table. —Compare TRUE COLOR, FALSE COLOR.

indirect object : —See INSTANTIATION.

indirect port : —See ACCELERATOR PORT.

infinity optics *n.* : Optical apparatus for producing a display wherein the image, as judged by the focus of the viewer's eyes, appears to be far distant. The effect is to enhance the realism and to reduce eyestrain, as the eye muscles are at rest when focused at a distance. In such displays the focus may actually be at a finite distance, at 30 feet, for example.

Initial Graphics Exchange Specification : —See IGES.

ink-jet printing : A means of printing in which droplets of ink are controlled and directed at paper so that an image is formed by the pattern of successive drops.

input-indexed color : A variation of indexed color in which colors are looked up and converted to true color prior to storing them in a frame buffer.

instancing *n.* : —See INSTANTIATION.

instantaneous field-of-view : —See FIELD-OF-VIEW.

instantiation [*alt.* instancing] *n.* : Reuse of a portion of a graphics database by reference to a common model at different locations. For example, the graphics database description of a fastener might be reused many times in a mechanical CAD database. Also called the use of *indirect objects*.

Institute of Electrical and Electronic Engineers : —See IEEE.

instruction stream : A set of instructions or commands that must be executed serially, although these instructions may bc executed on different processors.

Intel, Inc. : Santa Clara, CA, major semiconductor manufacturer, producer of the i860™ processors widely used in graphics accelerators, as well as microprocessors for personal computers, including the Pentium™

intensity *n.* : —See BRIGHTNESS

interactive *adj.* 1 : Being processed at a rate sufficiently fast to allow a user to make changes while working on-line with a system. For manipulating three-dimensional graphics, an update rate of about five frames per second is about the lower limit for interactive operation. For other types of activities, response times of several seconds up to perhaps a minute or two, for infrequent operations, may suffice as interactive. —Compare *real time.* 2 : On-line, as opposed to being in batch mode.

interglyph *adj.* : —See GLYPH.

interlace *n.* : A system of video display in which odd and even numbered scanlines are displayed on successive fields.

Interleaf : A word processing and desktop publishing system.

interleaving *n.* 1 : A technique for increasing the rate at which data can be read or written to digital memory by organizing the memory in sections that can be accessed in parallel or overlapping time slots. 2 : In television video, the technique for transmitting chrominance and luminance signals within the same frequency band.

internal test : In JTAG scan-path testing, a mode whereby the diagnostic hardware is able to supply a stimulus to the input pins of a target module, and after X clocks sample the resultant data on the output pins; called *internal* because the module can be tested in isolation.

International Standards Organization : —See ISO.

Internet : A worldwide digital data network originally sponsored by the U.S. government's Defense Advanced Research Projects Agency.

internetworking *n.* : The technology of communication among different networks.

interocular distance *n.* : The spacing between the eyes, usually as related to the adjustment of display apparatus having two eyepieces.

interpenetration *n.* : The arrangement of two or more graphics objects so that surfaces of the objects mutually intersect; the intersection may not be specified explicitly, but rather shown as a result of a z-buffered or other rendering. Also, **interpenetrate** *v.i.* : to be in the state of interpenetration.

interrupt *n.* : A means of initiating communication between a device and a processor, in which the device sends a signal to the processor that causes current processing to be suspended and a service routine to be initiated.

intersection *n.* : In constructive solid geometry, the region in three-dimensional space within both of two or all of three or more specified solid objccts. —Compare UNION.

interworking *n.* : Transparent sharing of resources and process-to-process communication over an interconnected system of computer networks.

invert *v.t.* 1 : To convert a logic value to its opposite, i.e., 0 to 1 and 1 to 0. 2 : To reverse the roles of black and white in an image.

IP *n.* 1 : *I*mage *P*rocessing. 2 : *I*nitial *P*osition; the starting conditions of a moving sequence or a flight simulation exercise.

Iris™ : A family of graphics workstations produced by Silicon Graphics, Inc.

IrisGL *Iris Graphics Language*; graphics interface for Silicon Graphics systems, uniform across their product line.

Iris Graphics, Inc. : Reading, MA, manufacturer of high-resolution large-format color ink-jet plotters.

IRIX™ *n.* : Silicon Graphics, Inc., version of UNIX having extensions for multiprocessing and real-time control.

ISDN *I-S-D-N*\\ : *I*ntegrated *S*ervices *D*igital *N*etwork; network standard allowing voice and data to share lines in an office environment. (The standard joke is that it stands for "*I S*till *D*on't *N*eed it.")

ISO *I-so*\\ : *I*nternational *S*tandards *O*rganization; international organization including groups establishing standards for graphics, image processing, and telecommunications.

isometric projection : A perspective projection in which vertical lines remain vertical.

isosurface *n.* : A surface defined by a function of three-dimensional space being equal to a constant, particularly in the context of visualizing physical properties such as temperature, density, stress, or the like.

isotropic radiation : Light from an idealized source emitting equal intensity in all directions.

ISV *I-S-V*\ : *Independent Software Vendor*; a maker of software products not owned by the company manufacturing the hardware on which the software runs.

IU *I-U*\ : *Integer Unit*; the integer arithmetic processing unit in a workstation

J

jack in [similar to *plug in*, a *jack* being a connector receiving a plug; the connotation is not, as some have supposed, obscene] *v.t.* : To communicate by engaging an information source, especially an electronic source such as a computer bulletin board.

jaggies [*slang*, from *jagged edges*] [*pl.* but used as singular in construction] *n.* : Aliasing artifacts in a rendered image, particularly stairstepping.

jittering *n.* : A means of antialiasing by stochastic sampling in which the sample point locations are obtained by adding a small noise component to nominal values on a subpixel grid. Also, **jitter** *v.t.* : to apply jittering.

J-lead *adj.* : Related to an integrated circuit package for surface mounting in which short leads are folded in the shape of a "J" down the sides of the package and underneath it; harder to inspect solder joints.

join surface : BLEND SURFACE.

joint *n.* : The point at which two successive segments of a spline curve meet. The joint is in coordinate space while the corresponding *knot* is in parameter space.

Joint Photographic Experts Group : —See JPEG.

Joint Test Action Group : —See JTAG.

joystick [named by early, rude aviators] : A graphics input device in which left-to-right and front-to-back deflections of a vertical lever are translated into motions of a displayed graphics object. The simplest form of joystick, used for computer games and the like, provides only switch contact closures in typically the eight principal directions, with action being taken so long as the closures are held. A more elaborate form provides outputs proportional to the deflection in each axis, usually with separate *trim* controls to adjust the centered zero point. A *three-dimensional joystick* provides additional degrees of freedom by providing, for example, one or more rotating controls on the top of the stick. The more elaborate designs are not necessarily springloaded to return to a neutral position, but may be left in correspondence with the position or attitude of a graphics object. The military uses joysticks for flight control in which there is little or no motion of the stick; the applied control force is sensed by integral strain gauges.

JPEG \ *J-peg* \ : Joint Photographic Experts Group; an ISO standards committee.

JTAG \ *jay-tag* \ *n.* 1 : Joint Test Action Group; group authoring an industry standard for a scan-path testing methodology for electronic circuits and systems. 2 : The document "JTAG Boundary Scan Architecture Standard Proposal," March 1988 release.

justification *n.* : The process of vertically aligning text, usually for printing. Right justification, so that the last characters of text adjacent to the right margin are even, requires that the individual widths of characters and spaces be accumulated across the spaces, and additional space be added between characters or words, or both. Since left justification is standard, *justification is* sometimes used to mean *right justiftcation.*

justified *n.* 1 : Text produced by justification. 2 : Text that is right justified; vertically aligned to the right margin. Not justified is *ragged.*

K

K \K, or *kilo*- when used as a prefix\ *n.* 1 : In the context of computer storage, 1024 (= 2^{10}). For example, 4K bytes equals 4096 bytes. 2 : In the context of money, $1000. For example, $4K equals $4000.

kana *n.* : The collective term for katakana and hiragana.

kanji *n.* : A subset of Chinese pictographic characters used in modern written Japanese. About 3000 of the more than 10,000 Chinese characters are used. The minimum resolution for recognizable depiction of most characters is a bitmap of about 15 x 15, with higher resolution desirable.

katakana *n.* : The set of about 100 characters used in Japanese mainly for syllable-by-syllable transliteration of foreign words. —See also, HIRAGANA.

kermit *n.* : A program for communicating ASCII files between computers; versions exist in the public domain for many different computers, so it is sort of the lowest common denominator for such communication.

kernel *n.* : The portion of an operating system that provides overall control and basic capabilities such as process management, file system access, and communication facilities.

kerning *n.* : Reduction of the space between letters in typesetting so that portions of the letters overlap horizontally. Also, kern *v.t.* : to apply kerning.

WAVE   WA VE

Type with Kerning   Type without Kerning

key *n.* : The black primary in color printing. —See also, CMYK.

keyframe *n.* : In computer animation, one of a sequence of images, defined manually or interactively, from which additional intermediate images are derived automatically by computer to complete an animated sequence. —See also, INBETWEENING.

kinesthesia n. : The human awareness of motions and relative parts of the body. Also, **kinesthetic** *adj.* : related to the sensation of motion by humans.

78

kinetic depth effect : The impression of three dimensionality in the projected images of an object achieved by rotating the object about its central axis, so that perspective causes nearer portions of the object to move more quickly and in the opposite direction in screen space than distant portions.

knot *n.* : One of the points in parametric space that defines the partitioning of a spline curve. —Compare JOINT.

L

L* *L-star*\ : LIGHTNESS.

label *n.* : Descriptive text associated with a graphics object.

labial *adj.* : Related to lips; in the present context, most often to the functions of the lips in speech.

lacunarity [coined by Benoit Mandelbrot, from Latin *lacuna,* gap. c. *1977*] *n.* : The property of a fractal having large intervals, such as empty circular or spherical regions, so that it appears not to fill space. Also, **lacunar** *adj.* : being characterized by lacunarity. —Compare SUCCOLARITY.

ladder *n.* : In typesetting, a group of several consecutive lines each ending with a hyphenated word. Considered undesirable.

Lambert *n.* : —See FOOTLAMBERT, MILLILAMBERT.

Lambert's cosine law : Relationship stating that the light intensity reflected from a surface is proportional to the cosine of the angle between the vector to the light source from the surface and the surface normal. The law applies to diffuse reflectors, surfaces that appear like chalk.

laminate *n.* : A graphics construct involving surfaces intended to be truly coplanar, such as text upon a polygon surface; a structure of *nested faces*.

LAN \as a word, *lan,* like *land* without the "*d*"\ : Local Area Network; a computer network serving a relatively small geographic area, generally serving up to perhaps 50 or 100 users.

landscape mode : The orientation of a display screen or paper printout in which the long dimension is horizontal.

laser printer *n.* : A xerographic printer in which a print image is written on the print drum by scanned and modulated laser light : ELECTROPHOTOGRAPHIC PRINTER. —See also, XEROGRAPHY.

laser projector : A type of video projector in which a raster composed of the combined beams from three color-component-modulated lasers is scanned mechanically. Since the lasers produce spectral colors, the range of displayable colors (the *gamut) is* large, and the collimated beams produce an image that is in focus at all distances. While successfully prototyped, laser projectors have yet to see widespread commercial application.

latency *n.* : Delay between an event and the response to the event, such as between movement of a user's head and the corresponding change in the imagery appearing on the user's head mounted display.

layer *n.* : In two-dimensional graphics, a set of data logically associated for treatment as if it were one of a stack of overlays when presented graphically. For example, a layer of geographic map data containing roads, where other layers might contain bodies of water, man-made structures, and navigation routes.

layering *n.* : Organizing data in layers.

LCD : *L*iquid *C*rystal *D*isplay; a flat-panel display using a thin layer of a liquid sandwiched between two (typically) glass sheets. Application of voltage through transparent conductors to regions of the panel causes polar molecules in the liquid to align with the applied field, thereby changing the optical properties in those regions. Displays may be viewed by reflected light or by transmission from a separate back light. Color versions use color filters over small regions of the panel. [The redundant **LCD display** is common.]

leading [from the metallic element lead, as used in traditional typesetting] *n.* : The distance between lines of printed text, usually measured in points between the baselines of successive lines.

leaf *n.* : A display list or portion of a display list having no control elements determining data selection. *pl.* **leaves**.

LED *L-E-D*, or occasionally, *led*\ *n.* : *L*ight *E*mitting *D*iode; semiconductor device producing light over a small area, used typically for indicator lights and matrixed into small displays. Typically red, but available in yellow, green, and (most recently) blue; also in a type having color changing with applied voltage. Also, *adj.* : built with LEDs <LED display>.

Lempel-Ziv and Welch compression : —See LZW COMPRESSION.

leveling *n.* : In a large database of graphics, the replacement of a modeled object with a more or less detailed version, as a function of distance or projected size, to minimize the time spent on rendering small details. Common in flight simulator graphics.

level-of-detail : One of the models used in a sequence for leveling.

level-of-detail blending : The technique of overlaying two models in a level-of-detail sequence, with the transparency of the models controlled as a function of time so that one model is introduced by increasing its opacity from zero, and the other model is removed by decreasing its opacity to zero. The objective is to minimize the potential distraction of a sudden change in appearance when the level-of-detail is changed.

light *adj.* : Having a high color value : being closer to white than black.

lightness *n.* : A metric for the brightness component of a color used in the CIELAB color space; it is proportional to the cube-root of luminance (to yield approximately equal perceived changes in brightness for proportional changes in lightness) and normalized from 0 to 100. Thc conventional notation is L*.

light pen : Graphics input device used for selecting objects by directly pointing to them on the CRT screen; it works by timing the raster until it sweeps to the light sensor in the pen.

light point : In flight simulation graphics, a graphics object for simulating airport and other lights usually having fixed pixel dimensions and special rules for altering the brightness with distance and visibility.

light source : A modeled source of illumination for the rendering of a graphics image; see LOCAL LIGHT SOURCE, POINT LIGHT SOURCE, EXTENDED LIGHT SOURCE, DIRECTIONAL LIGHT SOURCE, AMBIENT LIGHT.

light valve : A type of video projector in which the intensity of a light source is modulated by a raster scanned device. The modulating device may be a liquid crystal, a crystal that has reflective properties changed by a scanned electron beam, or (in the oldest technology) an oil film whose refractive properties are changed by a scanned electron beam. Because, unlike a CRT, the light source is independent of the image, the projected imagery is potentially brighter.

line *n.* 1 : Usually in graphics, a segment of a straight line. 2 : A straight line in space of infinite extent. 3 : A curve in space.

linear depth cueing : Depth cueing in which the interpolation between object color and background (or fading) color is linearly proportionate to the distance, between preselected minimum and maximum distances. Minimum and maximum cueing proportions are fixed outside of the region of linear interpolation.

line art : Images consisting only of black and white elements, without halftoning or dithering.

line intersection model : An algorithm for rendering the overlap of two lines in a graphics system. One model is to add the intensities of the lines, mimicking a stroke-writing system. Another model is to have the nearer line occlude the farther.

line-of-sight : The direction of view used for a particular graphics image, i.e., the direction in which the virtual camera is pointed.

line style : The characteristic of a drawn line determined by a pattern of breaks, such as continuous, dotted, dashed, or various combinations of dots and dashes.

line width : The thickness of a drawn line, sometimes limited to an integral number of pixels on a display.

liquid crystal display : —See LCD.

listener distribution : A type of window system input management in which the window most recently specifically designated is given current input, also known as "click to type."

list priority algorithm : Any algorithm that assigns occlusion priorities to a set of graphics objects. Knowing the order in which objects occlude permits the hidden surface problem to be solved by various means, including the *painter's algorithm*.

local area network : —See LAN.

localization *n.* : the process of identifying the relative position on an object in space, such as the human sensory process of locating a sound source relative to the listener.

local light source : A source of illumination for the rendering of a graphics image modeled near the scene rather than at infinity, so that the light rays may not be considered as coming from the same direction for each point on each object.

lock height : The maximum distance above a digitizing tablet at which the puck or stylus will operate.

LOD : —See LEVEL-OF-DETAIL.

lofted surface *n.* : A surface created by lofting.

lofting *n.* 1 : Creating a ruled surface between two given curves. 2 : Defining a surface by interpolation among a set of curves, typically each curve being a cross section.

low-level : Having less abstraction; more like the format needed for execution on hardware. Thus, an assembly language is a low-level programming language, and low-level graphics software interfaces conform more closely to hardware dependencies than do high-level interfaces.

LSI \L-S-I\ : *L*arge *S*cale *I*ntegration; the class of integrated circuit devices having a complexity of roughly 200 to 2000 gates, or the equivalent. [Some sources extend the boundaries to well above 10,000 gates.]

LSSD \L-S-S-D\ : *L*evel-*S*ensitive *S*can *D*esign; a method of designing a circuit for automated diagnosis that involves providing an alternate serial shift path to latches so that the machine state can be read and reset independently in a diagnostic mode; LSSD is oriented toward the use of latches, in contrast to plain *scan design,* which uses registers.

lunch box : Lunch-box-sized external electronic package for peripheral equipment that cannot be accommodated within a workstation.

LUT *lut*\\ : *Look-Up Table*; a table, usually stored in hardware, dedicated to a particular application; it is hard to imagine a table in which things would not be looked up, so the term has redundancy.

Luv space *L-U-V*\\ : A rectangular coordinate space for specifying color and intensity designed so that small changes in each of the coordinates result in approximately the same amount of perceptual change to a human observer. Thus, for example, percentage errors in computing color components make sense when expressed in Luv space, but not in most other color spaces. The *L, u, v* components are linear transformations of the components from xyY *space.* —Compare CIELAB.

lux *n.* : A measure of luminous flux density, i.e., how much light strikes a surface per unit area, equivalent to one lumen per square meter or 10.76 footcandles.

LZW compression : *Lempel-Ziv* and *Welch* compression; a scheme for reversible compression of binary images in which codes are built adaptively to fit bit patterns encountered in the data. As with other binary compression methods, nonbinary images may be compressed by application of the method to each bit plane of the stored image. *GIF* and *TIFF* file formats are based on simple extensions to LZW compression.

M

M *mega-*\ 1 : In the context of computer storage, 1,048,576 (= 2^{20}). For example, 4M bytes equals 4,194,304 bytes. 2 : In the context of money, 1,000,000 (in the U.S.). For example, \$4M equals \$4,000,000.

Mac \mack\ : A Macintosh™ computer.

MAC : The file extension designating bit-mapped image files in a format compatible with Apple Computer's *MacPaint* program.

Mach banding : A visual illusion that occurs when too few intensity steps are used in the rendering of a continuously toned surface. The regions of constant intensity appear nonuniformly shaded with enhanced boundaries to adjacent regions, an illusion caused by the eye's special sensitivity to edgelike discontinuities. It is sometimes called a Venetian blind effect. To achieve a continuous appearance, either smaller-intensity steps must be used or the image must be computed with dithering.

Macintosh™ [the developer's misspelling of *McIntosh*, a type of apple, has been preserved in the product name] : Apple Computer's line of personal computers, noted for featuring a graphics user interface.

macroparallelism : The approach to parallel processing in computer systems in which entire processors are replicated as subsystems. —Compare MICROPARALLELISM.

magenta *n.* : One of the primary colors for color printing; approximately purplish-red. Also, *adj.* : magenta-colored.

magnify *v.t.* : [image processing] To enlarge an image without rotation, often by a power of two using pixel replication.

management *n.* : The set of activities associated with translating ambiguous requirements into well-defined tasks.

manipulandum *n.* : A device, to be grasped by a user, for connection to a force feedback simulator; "A force-reflecting mechanical interface: essentially a joystick that enables a human operator to interact with dynamic systems, virtual or real, through the haptic sense." Millman, P.A., et. al., "Design of a High Performance Haptic Interface to Virtual Environments," IEEE Virtual Reality Annual International Symposium, Seattle, WA, 1993.

manipulator *n.* : A robotic arm composed of rigid links connected by joints for grasping, moving, or otherwise interacting with objects under remote control.

Manufacturing Automation Protocol : —See MAP.

MAP *map*\ : *M*anufacturing *A*utomation *P*rotocol; standards for networking for computerized manufacturing.

map *v.* 1 : To project a two-dimensional pattern or image from the space in which it is defined onto flat or curved surfaces. If the pattern space is parallel to the surface, the resulting texture or image is said to be *surface mapped*—it appears as if it were applied like wallpaper. If the pattern space is parallel to a horizontal plane and mapped onto various polygons representing terrain, then it is said to be *ground mapped*. Also, *n.* : A file used in the administration of a network that holds the list of user passwords, the names of the machines on the network, or similar information.

marker *n.* : A typically small graphics object that does not obey all the laws of perspective, such as an icon that changes location but not size, and is usually clipped with a "hot-spot clip test"; typically used to mark points of interest in three-dimensional models.

mask *n.* 1 : A pattern of bits determining the inclusion of data, typically with a bit-by-bit logical AND operation. Also, *v.* 1 : To apply a mask to data. 2 : To designate portions of an image for subsequent editing operations or for protection from editing operations.

maskable *n.* : Preset, usually via hardware state, so that certain bits of incoming data are ignored, as prescribed by a pattern of bits. For example, data written to a frame buffer might be *maskable* so that only the green color component is written during a certain set of writes.

matte object : A graphics object rendered as pure black (and without shading) with the objective of leaving blank space for the later insertion of an image by compositing.

M-bus : SPARC CPU-to-memory bus, designed for plug in of CPU and memory modules parallel to a motherboard. Defined by industry consortium; Level 1 for single processors and Level 2 for multiprocessors.

MCAD : *M*echanical *C*omputer-*A*ided *D*esign; the market related to the design of mechanical structures and assemblies.

MCAE : *M*echanical *C*omputer-*A*ided *E*ngineering; the market related to the design and analysis, particularly analysis of stress and materials properties, of mechanical assemblies.

MDE : LSI Logic's *M*odular *D*esign *E*nvironment for designing gate arrays.

mechanical *n.* 1 : The mechanical components associated with an electronic assembly. 2 : In traditional typography, the completed paste-up of a page.

mechanical computer-aided design : —See MCAD.

mechanical computer-aided engineering : —See MCAE.

mechanism *n.* : In a graphics application interface, the underlying means by which policy is implemented.

medical imaging : The application of image processing techniques to medicine, including the processing and display of data from computed tomography and magnetic resonance scanners.

medium *n.* 1 : The base material upon which information is written or otherwise recorded, such as magnetic diskette, optical disk, or film. *pl.* **media.** 2 [*alt.* media] : A style or system of presenting information characterized by the mechanism of transmission, such as audio, video, or print.

megaflops *n.* : —See MFLOPS.

menu *n.* : A list of choices controlling the operation of a computer program, usually presented in boxed outline with selection made by a mouse. **Pull-down menus** appear in correspondence with the selection of headings from a list arrayed horizontally. **Pop-up menus** appear upon entry of a key sequence or mouse selection within a particular region of the screen. **Walking menus** provide additional menus of choices arrayed horizontally as selections from previous menus are made.

menu-driven *adj.* : Controlled by selecting items from menus, as opposed to entering commands by keyboard.

mesh *n.* 1 : A graphics object composed of polygons, typically triangles or quads, that share vertices and edges, and thus may be transmitted in a compact format to a graphics accelerator. 2 : A two-dimensional array of adjoining bicubic patches : bicubic mesh.

metaball [originated by K. Omuraetal] *n.* : A generalization of an algebraic surface related to a *blob,* but using superposed piecewise quadratic functions rather than exponentials. Used as a modeling primitive for ray tracing.

metafile *n.* : A file in a format designed for machine independence, such as a GKS *metafile.*

metamer *n.* : One of the color samples making up a *metameric match.*

metameric match : Two or more colors that appear identical to a human observer, even though the distribution of light energy among wavelengths may differ for each.

MFLOPS *megaflops*\\ *n.* : Million *F*loating-*P*oint *O*perations *P*er *S*econd; a measure of computational performance. Numbers cited are usually the peak performance, the maximum possible assuming data are supplied to every processing unit whenever needed.

MHEG : *Multimedia/Hypermedia Experts Group;* an ISO standards committee.

Micro Channel : IBM proprietary 32-bit bus for personal computers, available to other vendors by license.

microfacet *n.* : A surface facet on the scale of the roughness of a surface assumed for theoretical purposes. Various models of surface reflectance, particularly diffuse reflection, are derived from assumed distributions of microfacets.

microparallelism *n.* : In a computer or other digital processor, concurrent processing achieved by performing multiple operations within a single processor, for example, by having operations controlled by fields in a long instruction word. This is in contrast to **macroparallelism,** the approach in which whole processors are replicated.

millilambert *n.* : Unit of luminance measure, equal to 0.3142 nit. —See also, FOOTLAMBERT.

minify [image processing] *v.t.* : To reduce the size of an image, often by a power of two by averaging square groups of pixels. Usage parallels magnify : **minification, minified.**

mip map [coined at New York Institute of Technology from "*multum in parvo*," Latin "many things in a small place," c. 1978] : Means of arranging the storage for a three-color-component zoom pyramid into a rectangular array of values. Successive resolutions of each color component require one-quarter of the storage space of the previous, allowing for tight packing of the data into storage. —See also, ZOOM PYRAMID.

Mip Map:
Successive resolutions of red (R0,R1,R2 …), green (G0,G1, G2 …), and blue (B0,B1,B2 …) color components of an image are packed in a square array.

MIPS : *Million Instructions Per Second;* a measure of computer system performance, limited in part by lack of consensus as to what constitutes an instruction, but including basic operations like LOAD and STORE.

MIPS Computer Systems, Inc. : San Jose, CA, manufacturer of RISC processor chips and workstations.

mirroring *n.* : In a drawing system, a feature allowing automatic creation of a new version of an existing graphics object where the new version is reflected symmetrically with respect to a prescribed line. Sometimes the feature is restricted to just a left-to-right reflection.

mission rehearsal system *n.* : A simulator used for practicing a specific future operation to be carried out in the real world, especially a military mission. A military mission rehearsal system generally provides higher realism, including more detailed imagery, than simulator systems used for generic training, and is therefore typically an expensive high-end system. Systems used for practicing a surgical procedure for a specific patient are among other applications in the broad *mission rehearsal* category.

miter *n.* : Treatment of thick lines meeting at a corner so that each line is beveled to make the join. Also, *v.t.* : to make a mitered joint; **mitered** *adj.* : meeting at a miter

Not Mitered   Mitered

MMU : *M*emory *M*anagement *U*nit, specialized hardware in a computer, which controls the access and swapping of data in a memory hierarchy, such as local memory to disk.

MMU page : A block of memory treated as a unit for management purposes by the MMU.

model *n.* : A collection of graphics objects in a database hierarchy, comparable to a *cluster* or PHIGS *structure*.

modeling *n.* : Activities related to the construction of a graphics database, as distinct from the *rendering* processes for producing images from a database.

modem *n.* : *mo*dulator-*dem*odulator; an electronic device that uses data to control the frequency, pulse width, or other characteristic of a nominal carrier signal for transmission and recovers data upon reception, especially a device for communicating computer data over telephone lines.

modulation transfer function : —See MTF.

moiré pattern *mwah-ray*\ : A global pattern that results from the addition of two or more patterns, each having fine detail approximately the same scale. In computer graphics, moiré patterns sometimes appear as an unintended result of operations carried out on the pixel level interacting with graphics, data having details with approximately pixel spacing. As such, the moiré patterns are an *aliasing* effect, and patterns of fine concentric circles or radially converging lines are used to test *antialiasing* algorithms.

molecular *adj.* : With reference to the state of a computer processor, requiring more than one instruction to update.

molecular modeling : An application of computer graphics for the interactive manipulation of images representing atoms and molecules, such as to determine the interaction of molecular structures. The graphics requirements often include *knobs* and *dials* for input, and require rendering of *spheres, dot clouds,* and *ribbons.* Stereo viewing is often used as well.

monochromatic *adj.* 1 : Having a single color, with reference to a display having a single phosphor producing either white, green, or amber. 2 : Having light energy at a single frequency of the spectrum, as produced by a laser.

monohedral tiling *n.* : A tiling of a plane by repeated use of a single geometric figure, possibly in different orientations.

morphing \presumably fr. *metamorphosis*\ *n.* : Changing from one dissimilar image to another, such as from an image of an animal to an image of a vehicle, in an animated sequence that shows a continuous gradual progression of changes.

motherboard : A printed circuit board having both its own circuitry and connector for plugging in additional boards. Small plug-in boards are *daughter boards.*

Motif : A graphics user interface proposed as a standard by the Open Software Foundation.

motion base *n.* : Mechanical apparatus that supports and moves a simulator cab or other simulator structure to provide kinesthetic cues to simulator users. Typically, the motion base has a limited range of motion, from a few centimeters to a few meters, that precludes sustained acceleration.

motion blur : Generation of motion-related blurred edges on moving objects in a graphics image so as to better preserve the illusion of continuous motion of the objects in an animated sequence.

MOTIVE : A CADDs tool for analyzing the timing effects of the physical layout of a printed circuit board; features a challenging user interface.

Motorola, Inc. : Schaumburg, IL, manufacturer of microprocessors, RISC processors, workstations, and other electronics products.

mottle *n.* : Unintended gross variations in intensity of a printed image. Also, *adj.* : **mottled.**

mouse *n.* : A graphics input pointing device having a mechanism for transmitting relative movements that are ultimately translated to changes in cursor position. One kind of mouse uses a rubber ball to transmit the horizontal and vertical motion of the device on a surface to two independent orthogonal directional sensors. An optical mouse works by detecting horizontal and vertical rulings on a prepared surface. There are typically one to three buttons on the mouse used to trigger events. Note that a mouse transmits changes in position, whereas a *digitizer* transmits absolute coordinates on a tablet.

MOVIE.BYU *movie dot B-Y-U*\\ [originated by H. Christiansen] : A computer graphics animation software package originated at Brigham Young University in Utah.

Moving Picture Experts Group : —See MPEG.

MP : —See MultiProcessor.

MPEG *M-peg*\\ : Moving Picture Experts Group; an ISO standards committee.

MR scanner : Magnetic Resonance scanner; a device for producing medical imaging data that uses radio-frequency energy to probe the properties of atoms in a strong magnetic field. Also **MRI** : Magnetic Resonance Imaging, the process including display of the data.

MS-DOS™ *M-S dahs*\\ : MicroSoft Disk Operating System; —See DOS.

MSI *M-S-I*\\ : Medium Scale Integration; the class of integrated circuits having roughly 20 to 200 gates, or the equivalent complexity. [The bounds vary by a factor of two or more, depending upon the source.]

MSP : The file extension designating bit-mapped image files in a format compatible with the personal computer *Microsoft Paint* program.

MT : *Material Transfer*; —See IMT.

MTF : *Modulation Transfer Function*; for a graphics display, the ratio of output amplitude to input signal amplitude as a function of frequency.

Multibus : An industry standard bus architecture, principally for workstations and industrial products, extended to 32 bits as **Multibus II** (standard IEEE 1296).

multimedia *adj.* 1 : Having more than one means of conveying information, such as text with sound or video. 2 : Related to a product for playback on a computer distributed on CD-ROM and having text, static images, sound clips, and video clips. Also, *n.* : The integration of video and sound into the workstation environment. More generally, the integration of two or more forms of electronically reproducable material.

Multimedia/Hypermedia Experts Group : —See MHEG.

multimodal *adj.* 1 : Having different means or characteristics of operation, such as having a search mode and a track mode. 2 : Having inputs for two or more of the senses.

multiplexor *n.* : An electronic circuit with one data input and more than one data outputs, with a control signal that determines which data output will receive the data input. Also, **multiplex** *v.t.* : to switch among signals or to share.

multiprocessor *adj.* : Having more than one processing unit, generally, running the same or similar instruction sets and sharing computational work.

multi-tasking *n.* : Executing more than one computer program concurrently by switching a processor among them sequentially.

Munsell color system : A system for specifying colors according to Munsell hue, chroma, and value. A cylindrical coordinate system is used with hues (red, orange, yellow, etc.), arranged by angle, chroma by radial distance (pastel to saturated), and value by z-axis distance (dark to light). Use of the system is enhanced by publication of books of carefully prepared classified color samples to which an unknown may be matched by eye. The system is designed to provide equal perceptual changes for constant increments in each coordinate.

mux *mucks*\\ [*slang*] *n.* : A multiplexor. Also, **mux** *v.t.* : to multiplex.

N

NAND *nand*\\ [all caps. consistent with AND and OR logic functions] *n.* 1: Not *AND*; a logic function in which the output is true if one of two inputs is false. 2 : The result of applying the NAND function <C is the NAND of signals A and B>. Also, *v.t.* : To perform the NOR function. Also **NANDs, NANDed, NANDing.**

NAPLPS *nap lips*\\ : North American Presentation-Level Protocol Syntax; a standard object-oriented graphics ASCII character file format used mainly for *videotex*. ANSI standard X3.110-1983.

navigation *n.* : Traditionally, the process of getting from place to place using a means of positioning and a means of steering (piloting); sometimes loosely used to refer only to a means of location in a virtual world, more in the sense of *orientation*.

NCGA : National Computer Graphics Association; organization for computer graphics, holding East Coast and West Coast conferences each year. More applications oriented than SIGGRAPH.

NC programming : Numerical Control programming; the programming of a digitally controlled machine tool to fabricate a part, often with the use of computer graphics to visualize the tool motion sequence.

NDC : Normalized Device Coordinates; —See NORMALIZED.

nested face [flight simulator graphics] : A polygon coplanar with another polygon, usually inheriting some of the attributes of the polygon upon which it is nested. —Compare LAMINATE.

net list : For an electronic circuit board, a tabular listing of the wired interconnections associated with each component pin.

net user : A graphics system that runs software on a machine other than the one with the display device and accesses graphics devices only over the network.

network *n.* : Electronic communication means for interchanging digital data among computers and related hardware, typically by multiplexing data over at most a few wires or optical fibers.

Network File System : —See NFS.

Newman and Sproull : The classic text by William Newman and Robert Sproull: *Principles of Interactive Computer Graphics*, 2nd ed., McGraw-Hill, New York, 1979.

NeWS™ [Sun Microsystems, Inc.] : Network Extensible Window System; window system based on PostScript proposed by Sun as an industry standard.

NeXT, Inc. : Company started by ex-Apple founder Steve Jobs, producing workstation systems initially aimed at the college-level education market.

NFS™ : Network File System; widely adopted software standard for sharing files among dissimilar computers over a network. Originated by Sun Microsystems, Inc.

nibble [half a byte; *alt.* nybble] *n.* : Four bits grouped as a unit for storage and processing. Generally aligned as halves of a byte.

nit [from Latin, *nitere*, to shine] *n.* : A unit of luminance, i.e., photometric brightness of a surface, equal to a candela per square meter or 0.2919 footlamberts. The nit is the preferred unit of brightness in international standards.

non-linear mapping : Transformation of an image in which the projection scale or rotation varies over the image as required, for example, to distort an image to compensate for projection through a fisheye wide-angle lens.

nonuniform *adj* : Having unequally spaced subdivisions, as a nonuniform spline in which the knots are unequally spaced. Equally spaced subdivisions are *uniform*.

NOR [see *AND* for use of all caps.] *nor*\ *n.* 1 : A logic function in which the output is true if none of two or more inputs is true. 2 : The result of applying the NOR function <C is the NOR of signals A and B>. Also, *v.* : To perform the NOR function. NORs, NORed, NORing.

normal *adj.* : Perpendicular to a surface. *n.* : The normal vector, a unit vector orthogonal to the tangent plane of a differentiable surface at a specified point. In graphics, the surface may be a conceptual underlying surface rather than the one actually modeled; for example, for a sphere approximated by polygons the normals may be taken to the original sphere rather than the polygonal approximation. —See also, FACE NORMAL, VERTEX NORMAL.

normalized *adj.* : Scaled to a predetermined value or range. A **normalized vector,** also called a **unit vector,** is scaled so its length is one. **Normalized device coordinates** are used within a graphics system for processing convenience and, usually, involve scaling input, output, or processed data to the range 0 to 1.

NPI *N-P-I*\ : New Product Introduction procedure; a procedure giving the requirements for new product development and transitioning to manufacturing. Also, *adj.* : related to new product introduction.

NTSC \N-T-S-C\ : National Television Standards Committee; the standard for the color-encoding of television video used in North America, parts of South America, and Japan. (The standard joke is that it means Never Twice the Same Color.)

NTSC encoder : A device that accepts RGB video signals plus a composite sync signal and produces an NTSC-compatible composite video signal.

Nubus : An I/O bus standard originated by Apple Computer for Macintosh II computers and offered as an industry standard, IEEE 1196.

NURB \nurb\ n. : Non-Uniform Rational B-spline; mathematical description of a curved surface. In each region of the spline, the surface is specified as a ratio of two polynomials. Also, adj. : Being composed of a NURB <a NURB surface>.

nybble n. : Common alt. of NIBBLE. [The two spellings are used about equally often.]

O

OA \ *O-A* \ : *Office Automation*; the computer and computer graphics application segment dealing with business applications, especially activities such as document preparation and distribution, which were not traditionally automated.

object *n.* : —See GRAPHICS OBJECT.

object-oriented *adj.* 1 : Composed of mathematically described graphics objects rather than of bit-mapped images. 2 : Using a programming style dealing with data objects having prescribed attributes.

object space : The coordinate system in which a graphics object is defined.

occlusion : The aspect of graphics image processing that deals with objects nearer to an observer covering those that are farther away; some prefer to call this *occultation*.

occlusion mask : A pattern of bits, each corresponding to a subportion of a pixel, used to indicate which portions have been covered : BED OF NAILS.

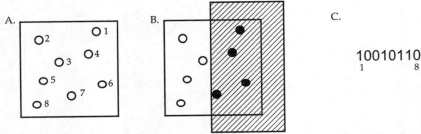

Occlusion Mask: Sample points within a pixel are numbered (A) so that those covered by a face (B) are associated with bits in an occlusion mask (C)

occultation : —See OCCLUSION.

OCR \ *O-C-R* \ : *Optical Character Recognition*; the process of converting scanned images of text into the codes for the alphanumeric characters for the text.

octal *n.* : The base-eight number system, useful for computers because each octal digit [0, ..., 7] corresponds to a pattern of three bits. Also, *adj.* : Being in octal.

96

octant *n.* : One of the eight subdivisions of the x-y plane produced by sub-dividing by the coordinate axes and by the lines x = y and x = -y. The eight cases are sometimes relevant to the design or testing of graphics algorithms.

octet [used mainly in defining network protocols, where the size of bytes may vary] *n.* : An eight-bit byte.

octree *ahk-tree*\ *n.* : A tree-structured subdivision of three-dimensional space in which a cube is recursively subdivided into eight equally sized cubes, down to smallest-sized cubes called *voxels*.

odd-even rule : WINDING RULE.

OEM *O-E-M*\ : Original Equipment Manufacturer; a company that builds electronic assemblies from components.

ONC™ : Open Network Computing; Sun Microsystem's network software comprising remote procedure calls (RPC) and external data representation (XDR) allowing computers to initiate processing and pass data over a network.

one-sided surface : A two-sided surface that is rendered normally when one side is facing the viewpoint and omitted from the rendering when the other side is facing the observer. Commonly used for terrain, for example, where the interesting renderings are all above the surface. —See also, BACKFACING.

opcode *n.* : The portion of a digital instruction for execution in hardware that specifies the type of operation to be performed rather than, for example, the location of the data upon which the operation is to be performed. For a computer a typical opcode might correspond to ADD; for a graphics accelerator, DRAW LINE.

open *adj.* : Of a graphics object, having a surface both sides of which may be viewed from potential viewpoints of interest. For example, a bowl modeled with a single surface.

OPEN LOOK™ [AT&T] : A graphics user interface specification originated by Sun Microsystems, Inc.

Open Software Foundation : —See OSF.

open system : A computer system in which the main components of the system architecture, as well as the software and hardware interfaces, are made available to outside developers of compatible equipment and software. Generally, an open system is capable of being cloned. The opposite is a *closed* or *proprietary* system.

Open Systems Interconnection : —See OSI.

optical character recognition : The processing of a digitized image of a document to recognizing printed letterforms and convert them to characters. —See SCANNER.

OR \or\ [see *AND* for discussion of all caps usage] *n.* 1 : A logic function in which the output is true if any of two or more inputs are true. 2 : The result of applying the OR function <C is the OR of signals A and B>. Also, *v.* : To perform the OR function. ORs, ORed, ORing.

ordinate *n.* : The y component of an (x,y) coordinate pair. The x component is the *abscissa*.

ornament *n.* : In typography, a small stylized artwork for inclusion with text.

orphan *n.* : In publishing, a heading or single line of text separated from its associated paragraph by a page break or column end.

orthographic projection : A projection from three dimensions to two dimensions without perspective division, so that objects do not shrink with distance.

OS/2™ \O-S-two\ : Microsoft Corp. developed operating system for IBM's PS/2 series of personal computers.

OSF \O-S-F\ : *Open Software Foundation*; An organization formed by a group of computer companies, including Hewlett-Packard, DEC, and IBM, to develop versions of UNIX not controlled by AT&T and Sun.

OSI \O-S-I\ : *Open Systems Interconnection*; a conceptual model for data communication and networking supported by ISO standards. The model features network layers providing services; the layers are: application, presentation, session, transport, internet and network, data link and medium access, and physical.

outline font : Letterforms defined by enclosing curves rather than by bit maps, so that they may be scaled and rotated without the resolution limits of a bit map. The fonts are conventionally rendered with solid fill, not necessarily as outlines.

overlay *n.* 1a. : A graphics image superimposed over a portion of another image, as, for example, a temporary "pop-up" menu over a graphics window. *v.t.* 1b : To superimpose. *n.* 2a. : A portion of a computer program that is loaded into memory and executed when requested by the portion of the program previously loaded. *v.t.* 2b: To load an overlay.

overlay planes : Additional frame buffer memory planes used so that an overlayed image may be displayed temporarily without rewriting the underlying main image when the overlay is removed.

oversampling *n.* : —See SUPERSAMPLING.

P

P0 *P zero*\ : A partial prototype of a new device, perhaps with major components missing, but suitable for debugging aspects of the product.

P1 *P one*\ *n.* 1 : The first engineering prototype of a new product, ready for debugging. 2 : The connector on a VME-bus backplane that is reserved for the standard VME bus connections. 3 : A time-honored yellow-green phosphor formulation used for CRT displays. The P1 phosphor can be driven to produce very high display brightnesses, so it is also used in specialized applications, such as cockpit displays that must be able to be viewed in sunlight. Designated GJ in the new WTDS system of phosphor identification.

P2 *P two*\ *n.* 1 : The debugged engineer prototype of a new product, ready for transition to manufacturing. 2 : The sccond connector on the VME-bus backplane; used for proprietary bus connections.

P3 *P three*\ *n.* : The third connector on a VME backplane, used for proprietary bus connections.

P4 *P four*\ *n.* : A phosphor formulation used for black-and-white television.

P22R, P22G, P22B *P-twenty-two-R, etc.* \ *n.* : The original designation of the phosphors for color television, now collectively designated as X.

packet *n.* 1 : A *parcel.* 2 : In data communications, a set of data typically having a descriptive header determining the size, routing information, and the like.

page description language : A specialized computer language for determining the appearance of a printed page, including features for specifying resolution-independent imagery. Typically, a dedicated processor in a laser printer or photo typesetting machine converts the description into print imagery.

paint *adj.* 1 : Of or related to a graphics software interface that employs the "move-draw" style of commands, such as would logically be used with a penplotter. 2 : Modifying pixels through user commands, as in a *paint program.*

painter's algorithm : A solution of the hidden surface problem in which objects are rendered in a frame buffer in an order such that higher-priority nearer objects are written over lower-priority objects. Roughly speaking, nearer objects are painted over more distant ones.

paint program : A program for creating raster images, usually in color, interactively, wherein the image is written directly to a frame buffer without separately retaining geometric figures that can be edited and redrawn. The style of interaction typically corresponds more closely to traditional drawing and painting than to drafting.

paint system : A system dedicated to operation of paint software, with output devices for video or hard copy.

PAL *pal*\\ *n.* 1 : *Phase Alternate Line*; the standard for the color encoding of television video used in most of Europe (excepting France) and much of the rest of the world apart from North America and Japan. Also, *adj.* : related or conforming to the PAL format. 2 : *Programmable Array Logic*; a method for implementing combinational logic circuits in a configurable device.

pale *adj.* : Having low color saturation : being closer to white than to a pure color.

palette *n.* : The range of colors available for selection by a graphics application. In indexed color systems, the palette is typically larger than the number of colors concurrently used. For example, the user may be allowed to use 256 colors selected from a palette of 16 million.

pan *v.i.* : To change the view of a given database by changes in translation for two-dimensional database or changes in viewing angle for a three-dimensional database, but without changing scale or position, respectively. For hardware pan the image is precomputed and stored, and panning is accomplished by selection of a portion of the stored image.

pancake window : A relatively flat optical assembly fitting in front of a CRT display to collimate the image, so that it appears to be distant. Used in flight simulation.

pane *n.* : A region of a graphics window typically containing one or more *gadgets*.

parametric *adj.* : Usually with reference to a curve or surface, being defined in terms of parameters that generate coordinate values of the function for each set of values of the parameters. A simple example is a circle, which may be defined as the locus of points solving $x^2 + y^2 = 1$, or, in a parametric form with $x = \cos q$ and $y = \sin q$ for the parameter q varying from 0 to $2p$.

PARC *park*\\ : *Palo Alto Research Center*; Xerox Corporation research organization noted especially for contributions to the development of graphics user interfaces.

parcel *n.* : A collection of graphics primitives preprocessed for efficient rerendering with changed viewpoints; a compiled leaf of a display list. The concept is widespread, but there is no industry-standard terminology for it, similar to a PACKET, MACRO, or NON-EDITABLE SEGMENT.

particle system [originated by W. Reeves] : A computer graphics technique for modeling irregular objects, such as clouds, smoke, and water, in which an object is represented by a time-varying collection of particles. The creation, motion, and deletion of individual particles is controlled by stochastic processes that are parameterized to control the object's overall shape and appearance. The particles are graphics primitives similar to dots, which may be rendered with motion blur.

patch *n.* 1 : A subdivision of a complicated surface having simpler properties in its domain. 2 : A curved surface defined with boundaries, rather than over the whole functional space. 3 : A modification to software, usually implemented so that the original software need not be recompiled. Also *v.t.* : to modify using a patch.

patch cracking *n.* : Cracking in conjunction with the tesselation of patch surfaces due to vertex placement inconsistent with that of adjoining tesselated patches. —See CRACKING.

path *n.* : In a graphics system, a sequence of attributes and processing steps that remain as defaults until explicitly changed.

pattern *n.* : A two-dimensional arrangement of pixels, usually of two different colors, that is applied to fill a polygon or other graphics object in screen coordinates and is not changed with perspective; —Compare TEXTURE.

PCB : *Printed Circuit Board*; the circuit board without components. With components, it becomes a *printed circuit assembly*.

PCL : *Printer Control Language*; Hewlett-Packard–originated command interface for laser printers, widely supported by emulation.

PCX : The file extension designating bit-mapped image files in a format compatible with the default format of the personal computer program *PC Paintbrush*.

pedestal level : BLANKING LEVEL.

pel [used mainly in image processing, and of declining popularity, it seems] *n.* : *Pic*ture *el*ement or *pixel*.

pen-based *adj.* : Using a pen-like object, typically a stylus, for input to a computer in the manner of handwriting.

penetron *n.* : BEAM-PENETRATION DISPLAY CRT.

penumbra *n.* : The portion of a shadow produced by an extended light source corresponding to regions where part, but not all, of the light source is occluded by the shadowing object.

peripheral vision : The low-resolution regions of vision away from the direction of view. Peripheral vision, while lower resolution than the centered foveal vision, is more sensitive to motion and intensity changes. Display flicker is usually more noticeable in peripheral vision, for example.

perspective *n.* : The reduction of apparent linear dimension in proportion to distance when viewing three-dimensional objects.

perspective division *n.* : The division-by-z operation in the process of perspective projection.

perspective projection *n.* : The mathematical transformation of three-dimensional coordinates to two dimensions in which the horizontal and vertical coordinates (x and y) are divided by the depth coordinate (z).

PERT chart : *Program Evaluation and Review Technique* chart; a diagram used for planning the activities and events, i.e., milestones, of a project. Originally, events were symbolized by annotated circles or boxes and activities by lines leading to the events. Now the terminology is also applied to charts in which boxes represent the activities and lines the events; also known as an *activity network*.

PET scanner : *Positron Emission Tomography* scanner; a device producing source data for medical imaging.

PEX *pecks*\ *n.* 1 : *PHIGS Extension to X*; a protocol for a three-dimensional graphics extension to X11 based on PHIGS+. 2 : *Packet EXchange*; a message communication service in the Xerox Network Systems (XNS) architecture.

PGA *P-G-A*\ 1 : *Pin Grid Array*, a type of integrated circuit package having many vertical pins for through-hole circuit boards or socketing. 2 : *Professional Graphics Adapter*; an IBM-originated frame buffer design for personal computers.

PGL : The file extension often used to designate files in the *HPGL* format.

PHIGS *figs*\ *n.* : *Programmer's Hierarchical Interface for Graphics Systems*; a software interface standard including data structures for high-level three-dimensional applications.

PHIGS+ *figs plus*\ *n.* : Extension to the original PHIGS specification including more extensive lighting models.

Phong shading : [originated by Phong Bui Tong, 1975]: Illumination on a surface calculated by first computing a surface normal at each pixel to be rendered by linearly interpolating from the vertices of the triangle containing the point corresponding to the pixel. The Phong illumination model is then applied, which uses the cosine of the angle between the incident light and the viewing direction. Thc cosine is raised to a selected power, according to the shininess of the surface, to produce highlights corresponding to specular reflection. Phong shading is associated with realistic representation of glossy surfaces, but at high computational cost, which includes renormalization of the interpolated vector.

phot *n.* : A unit of illuminance equal to 0.0001 lux.

photomapping *n.* : Applying a photographic (or photographiclike artwork) image to a surface as a texture map. : CEL TEXTURE.

photometer *n.* : A device for measuring luminance. The device includes appropriate weighting for the spectral sensitivity of the human visual system.

photometric *adj.* : Related to measurements of light that take into account the properties of the human visual system, especially the spectral sensitivity.

photopic *adj.* : Related to color vision in relatively bright light, sensed by the cones in the retina of the eye.

photopic luminous efficiency function : The function giving the relative sensitivity of the human visual system as a function of the wavelength of light, under conditions bright enough to permit color vision.

photoplotter *n.* : A plotter that draws on photosensitive material with light, used to achieve accuracy and high definition of fine lines as required, for example, for printed circuit board artwork.

photo-realistic rendering 1 : Creating a realistic looking image from geometric data, often merged with image data. 2 : Graphics with the objective of producing images that look realistic; **realistic rendering.**

PIC 1 : The file extension designating bit-mapped image files in a format compatible with the personal computer program *PC Paint Plus*. 2 : The file extension designating object-oriented graphics files compatible with personal computer programs *Windows Draw!, Lotus 1-2-3*, and others.

pica *n.* : A typesetting measure equal to one-sixth of an inch.

pi-cell *n.* : An optical device for electrically controlling the polarization characteristics of light, typically as an element of a stereo or color display.

pi character : In typesetting, a nonalphanumeric character such as a star (✫) or bullet (•) : a dingbat.

pick-and-place *adj.* : Relating to the selection and movement of graphics objects in a scene.

pick aperture : The region around the cursor within which objects will be identified when picking is initiated.

pick-highlight cycle : The process by which a picked object is identified interactively to a user by altering the object's appearance on the display.

pick identifier : —See PICKING.

picking *n.* : Process by which the user points at an object in the display and thereby identifies it to the application program. The identification is accomplished through a number, the **pick identifier,** associated with each primitive or group of primitives by the application, and subsequently returned by the graphics system when the primitive is picked. Usually, picking is initiated by an event (such as clicking the mouse), and the image is rerendered to find the picked object. There are also **continuous picking** and **pick-while-rendering,** in which the object nearest the cursor is always selected or is selected whenever the image is updated, respectively. More than one object may be near the cursor, resulting in a **pick list** of objects, which is then generally interactively culled further. The implementation requires an association of the rendered object with a database object or group of objects. For **two-dimensional picking,** only unoccluded objects are identified, whereas for **three-dimensional picking** occluded objects are considered as well.

pick list : —See PICKING.

pick-while-rendering : —See PICKING.

PICT : *PICT*ure files; the file extension designating object-oriented graphics files compatible with many programs on the Apple Macintosh.

pie chart : A graph in which data values are depicted as proportionately sized segments of a circular region that represents the whole.

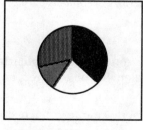

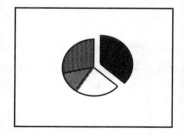

Pie Chart   Pie Chart with Exploded Wedge

pin grid array : A type of integrated circuit package having many vertical pins for through-hole circuit boards or socketing. This type of package typically provides the highest pin counts and best thermal characteristics of the alternatives currently available, but usually at added cost and with poorer electrical characteristics.

pinout *n.* 1 : Assignment of a package pin to each signal for an integrated circuit design. 2 : Specification of the function of each pin for an integrated circuit.

pipeline *n.* : Electronic circuitry in which successive sections of hardware perform successive processing operations, usually with registers or other storage elements buffering the data between sections. Processing occurs similar to manufacturing on an assembly line, with many operations occurring concurrently on different objects. Pipelined processing is used in many high-performance graphics and computer systems.

pipeline latency : The time required for a particular data item to complete all of the successive stages of a pipeline. This may be an important system consideration if the pipeline has to be drained to change processing parameters and subsequently refilled.

pitch *n.* : The angular displacement of a vehicle or device about the lateral axis, in the plane of the vertical and longitudinal axes.

pivot *v.i.* : To rotate with respect to a local origin.

pixel [from *picture element*] *n.* 1 : One of the individually addressable elements of an array of color or intensity data forming a digital image. 2 : The solid angle boundaries in space or the area boundaries in the projected image corresponding to the color and intensity values of an addressable point in a digital image. 3 : The smallest element on a raster display for which the color or intensity may be independently set. [Pixels need not necessarily be square or rectangular, although that is the overwhelming convention. Hexagonal pixels have been studied, for example.]

pixellization *n.* : A video special effect in which the image is converted to an array of square regions, like oversized pixels, with the values of color and intensity derived from the original image used uniformly in each region.

pixel perfection : Pertaining to which pixels are modified by graphics drawing operations, particularly as related to drawing compatibility with X.11, drawing compatibility across a product line, or drawing consistency within a product implementation.

pixmap *n.* : In the X Window System, a two-dimensional array of pixel data, with ich pixel having one or more assoc:ated bits. —Compare RASTER.

plan *n.* : A collection of well-defined tasks ordered by precedence, with each having defined resource requirements, an estimate of duration, and a defined output that marks completion.

planar *adj.* : Lying within a plane : flat.

plane 1 : —See BIT-PLANE. 2 : A mathematical plane, always of infinite extent.

plasma display : A flat-panel display in which information is presented by a matrix of cells capable of producing glowing dots by emissions of gas plasma, usually neon.

platform 1 : A baseline workstation, to which options are added to make a system. 2 : A baseline product of any kind, notably a software library.

PLCC : *Plastic Leadless Chip Carrier;* a type of integrated circuit package.

Plot3D : Program originated by NASA for the display of scientific data, widely used for computational fluid dynamics data. Also, the associated file format.

PNR : *Part Number Request;* the procedure used to establish approval for a new component not on the AVL, and to assign a part number.

PO : *Purchase Order;* the document sent from the purchasing department to the vendor to purchase the item requested via a purchase request.

point *n.* 1 : A location in space, specified by coordinates. 2 : In typesetting, the smallest unit of measure, equal to 1/72 of an inch.

point and shoot interface [*slang*] : A graphics user interface (*GUI*) featuring icons selected with a mouse.

pointer *n.* : In the X Window System, the input device currently controlling the position of the cursor.

pointing device : Graphics input hardware used to control the position of a cursor on the display, so as to point to an object in the displayed image. Pointing devices include *mice, digitizers,* and *track balls,* among others.

point light source : A light source modeled as if it radiates from a single point in space, either directionally or uniformly.

point sampling : Selecting the color and intensity for a pixel based upon the values of those parameters at a single point within the pixel, often, but not always, the center point. This method generally yields images having aliasing effects.

Polhemus Corp. : Colchester, VT, company manufacturing a system that concurrently determines the position and attitude of a sensor through the detection of electromagnetic fields. The system is applied to three-dimensional digitizing and to specialty applications such as head tracking for helmet-mounted displays in aircraft and simulators.

policy *n.* : The conceptual model presented by a program interface to a user, particularly as embodied by the specific semantics for its use. For example, the policy that the window with the cursor receives input events, versus the policy that the window to last register interest by receiving a mouse click (click to type) receives input events.

polling *n.* : A mechanism for initiating data transfer between two devices in which one of the devices makes periodic inquiries for the presence of new data.

polygon *n.* 1 : A closed nonintersecting geometric figure comprising an ordered set of coplanar vertices connected in sequence by sides and having a final side connecting the first and last vertices. 2 : In computer graphics, a generalized polygon. [Graphics usage is often casual about whether a traditional mathematically defined polygon is the subject of discussion, or the graphics-inspired generalization. The use of *generalized polygon* is encouraged whenever appropriate, to minimize this confusion.]

polygon converter model : Storage of spatial data, especially the outlines of map features, in which each entity is stored in a hierarchical data structure with pointers providing cross-references among entities.

polygon, generalized : A graphics figure comprising an ordered sequence of vertices, not necessarily coplanar, connected in sequence by sides that may intersect. A generalized polygon does not necessarily have a unique tesselation into triangles. A *two-dimensional generalized polygon* adds the constraint of coplanarity but does not prohibit self-intersection. Note that accumulated error in the transformation of coplanar vertices may produce noncoplanarity of practical consequence. If the polygon happens to be transformed to a view that is nearly on-edge, then self-intersection may be induced as well.

polyhedron [*pl.* polyhedra] : A closed three-dimensional graphics object composed of polygons, with each polygon edge shared by one other polygon, and each vertex shared by two or more polygons.

polyline : A series of connected line segments specified by an initial vertex, a sequence of vertices each defining the end of the previous segment and the start of the next, and a final vertex that ends the last segment. Also called a *vector chain*.

polymarker : A graphics object comprising a marker and a list of locations where the marker should be instantiated.

popping : In a moving sequence of graphics images, an undesired sudden change in the appearance of an object from one frame to the next. Popping may be attributed to an error in a culling algorithm or to too-aggressive level-of-detail adjustment.

pop-up menu : —See MENU.

port *v.t.* 1: To rewrite or adapt software written for a particular model of computer, operating system, or programming environment to run on another while preserving the original functionality. 2 *n.* : An interface between a host computer and a hardware device such as a frame buffer.

portal *n.* 1 : In a computer game, an entry into a different scenario usually represented by graphics depicting an entry and a sequence representing travel through a stylized passageway. 2 : In science fiction entertainment, a device for entering new scenes or changing locations.

Positron Emission Tomography scanner : —See PET SCANNER.

POSIX *poz-icks*\ [*P*ortable *O*perating *S*ystem *I*nterface + (for UNIX?)] : An IEEE committee and associated emerging set of standards designed to ensure the portability of software applications among various versions of UNIX and, potentially, to other multitasking operating systems as well.

posterization *n.* : Reducing the number of shades of gray or colors in an image so that the boundaries of gray shade or color regions are apparent, generally for artistic effect. Also, **posterize** *v.t.* : to apply posterization.

posting *n.* 1 : Initiating display list traversal. 2 : In PHIGS, associating a display list with a raster, but not initiating traversal.

POSTSCRIPT™ [Adobe Systems, Inc.] : A page description language created by Adobe Systems and widely used to drive laser printers; adopted as the basis of *NeWS*.

potentially visible : Related to a graphics object that must be processed for occlusion, regardless of whether it is ultimately completely occluded or not. Objects removed by culling or clipping are not regarded as potentially visible.

PowerGlove™ *n.* : Inexpensive dataglove used in a game system once manufactured by Nintendo, and still being adapted by hobbyists and researchers for experimentation.

PR *P-R*\ 1 : *P*urchase *R*equest; a form requesting the purchasing department in an organization to buy something. 2 : *P*ublic *R*elations; various activities related to publicity and corporate image. 3 : *P*ermanent *R*esidence; visa status allowing one to live and work in the U.S. without being a citizen.

Pratt : The standard text *Digital Image Processing* by William K. Pratt, John Wiley and Sons, New York, 1978.

preemptive scheduling : A means of scheduling the sharing of common computer or graphics resources in which user applications are forced to relinquish use of resources; currently rarely implemented in window systems.

primitive *n.* : One of the objects known by a graphics system and available to users for the construction of more complex graphics images. For example, most graphics systems have lines and triangles as primitives; a polygon might also be a primitive, or it might be left to the user to form a polygon from triangles. A system may include both geometric primitives and *raster primitives,* the latter including raster fonts and operations on pixel data.

Printer Control Language : —See PCL.

prioritization *n.* : The sorting of graphics objects into order of occlusion.

priority-ordered : Objects ordered from near to far for occlusion processing in the rendering of a graphics image; the presence of intersecting, concave, or cyclically overlapping objects may prevent priority-ordering.

prismatic joint *n.* : In a robotic manipulator, a joint that changes length, typically through a sliding mechanism.

procedural surface : Surfaces for graphics modeling defined implicitly, such as by sweeping a curve or solid through space or by intersecting simpler surfaces or solids.

process *n.* : A program while being executed, usually as one of several in a multiprogramming environment.

processor *n.* : Any hardware device capable of executing a sequence of predefined operations on digital data.

product specification : A document designed to describe all the features planned for a product as independently as possible from the means used to implement them.

product team : Collection of representatives from various organizations that meets to coordinate the introduction of a new product; includes representatives from the project, diagnostics, reliability, packaging, etc., as specified in the NPI Procedure.

Professional Graphics Adapter : —See PGA.

Programmable Read-Only Memory : —See PROM.

projection pipeline : The initial portion of the graphics pipeline, up to and including the transformation from three-dimensional world coordinates to two-dimensional screen coordinates.

PROM \prahm\n. : Programmable Read-Only Memory; digital memory that can be encoded with data by a user once, but thereafter cannot be reprogrammed.

proportional spacing : Property of text in which the widths of characters and the associated space allotted for each varies with the character.

proprietary adj. : Owned by a company and kept unavailable to others, except possibly for high licensing fees, through patents, copyrights, and trade secrets. The opposite of open.

protocol n. : Specification of the hardware and software interface to a bus or network.

prototile n. : One of the geometric figures used repetitively to tile a plane.

PS/2™ \P-S-two\ : IBM's series of personal computers featuring the Micro Channel™ Architecture.

pseudocolor n. : One of the colors resulting from pseudocoloring.

pseudocoloring n. : Application of colors to an image, typically using a color table, so that colors are used to represent data values other than the natural color of an object. For example, the intensities in a monochrome image may be mapped to colors as a way of making small changes in intensity more apparent. : colorizing. —Compare FALSE COLORING.

puck n. : The movable cursor assembly used with a digitizing tablet to accurately locate points for input.

pull-down menu : —See MENU.

purchase order : —See PO.

pure adj. : Appearing saturated in color : appearing monochromatic or spectral in color; undiluted by white.

purity n. 1 : The degree to which a region on display is correctly presented as being uniformly colored; especially on a shadowmask CRT having adjustment mechanisms for purity errors 2 : The degree to which a color is saturated; a completely pure color has light only at one frequency of the spectrum. Also, adj. : related to purity.

Purkinje effect : The loss of brightness of reds and oranges relative to blues and green at low light levels as the eye adjusts from day (scotopic) to night (photopic) vision.

Q

Q *n.* : The quadrature component of an encoded color video signal or the corresponding green-to-magenta component of a color coordinate space. —See YIQ SPACE.

QE : *Quality Engineering.*

quad *n.* : Quadrilateral, a graphics figure specified by a closed sequence of four vertices.

quad, convex : A planar quad in which any two points on the perimeter may be connected by a line entirely within the quad.

quad, generalized : A quad that may be nonplanar or self-intersecting.

Quads: (A) convex, (B) concave, (C) self-intersecting (bow tie),
(D) and (E) alternate triangularizations of convex quad

quadrant *n.* : One of the four quarters of the x-y plane produced when the plane is bisected by the x and y coordinate axes. Corresponds to the four cases of positive or negative x with positive or negative y, and hence provides four cases of line slopes that must be tested with a line-drawing algorithm.

quadric surface : Curved surface formed by the set of points satisfying a second-degree polynomial equation in three variables. Yields, depending upon the parameters : spheres, ellipsoids, cones, paraboloids, hyperboloids, and hyperbolic paraboloids.

quadrilateral : —See QUAD.

quad tesselation : Subdivision of a quad into two triangles.

quadtree *n.* : A tree structure organization of two-dimensional space, starting with a square and recursively subdividing each square into four equal squares, down to the smallest squares, pixels.

quality knob : A parameter or software switch controlled by the user of a graphics system to effect tradeoffs between rendered image quality and processing speed, for example, to turn antialiasing on and off.

quantization *n.* : The process of converting a signal or function that varies continuously over a range into discrete levels, usually a range of successive binary numbers starting at zero. *Linear quantization* puts the binary numbers in correspondence with equal intervals over the continuous range. *Nonlinear quantization* puts the numbers in correspondence with nonuniform intervals covering the continuous range. In graphics, having too few quantization levels for intensity, i.e., too few shades of gray, produces artifacts in the image such as *Mach banding*. Potential cures include increasing the number of bits per pixel, using nonlinear quantization, or dithering—or some combination of the three.

quantizer *n.* : A means of performing quantization, usually in hardware.

quartic surface : Curved surface formed by the set of points satisfying a third-degree polynomial equation; includes the surface of a torus.

QWERTY \as a word, *querty*\ : The traditional layout of keyboard, in which the letters Q-W-E-R-T-Y appear on the left of the top row of letters. The alternate *Dvorak* layout is proposed as a more efficient alternative, but its use is very rare.

R

radiometer *n.* : An instrument for measuring radiance, i.e., light intensity (in watts, for example), independent of the human visual system's sensitivity variations with wavelength. —See also, PHOTOMETER; PHOTOPIC LUMINOUS EFFICIENCY FUNCTION.

radiosity *n.* : An illumination algorithm for graphics that accurately computes the effects of diffuse illumination, including multiple diffuse reflections from surfaces, through an energy balancing technique.

RAMDAC *ram-dack*\\ *n.* : *R*andom *A*ccess *M*emory *D*igital-to-*A*nalog Converter; a DAC circuit element that additionally contains tables for translating input digital color values, as is needed for indexed color or gamma correction prior to display.

RAMdisk *n.* : A portion of a computer's random access memory dedicated to simulating a disk drive, thereby allowing software written to access disk memory to operate with much faster semiconductor memory.

random scan : The CRT scan system associated with a calligraphic display, as opposed to that of a raster scan display.

range contrast : —See CONTRAST.

raster *n.* 1 : A set of memory locations to be treated as pixels, residing either on the display device (as *display memory)* or in the memory system of the host computer that supports the display. If a raster is defined in host memory rather than display memory, at some point it will have to be transferred or mapped into display memory to be visible as an image. However, the facility of maintaining host-memory rasters is useful for many purposes, including the retention of images that are temporarily covered by a newly created window on the display. A raster may be irregularly shaped, defined either geometrically or by a bit map. 2. : The pattern of horizontal lines produced in a scanned CRT display. Also, *adj.* : related to being scanned horizontally and vertically, as a *raster* display.

raster coordinates : The coordinate system associated with a rectangular raster, typical with the origin in the upper left, x positive to the right, and y positive down.

rasterization *n.* : The process of generating individual pixels for a graphics image from graphics primitives.

rasterize *v.t.* : To divide into pixels : SCAN CONVERT.

raster-op *n.* : —See ROP.

raster operation : —See ROP.

raster text : Text defined by a pattern of pixels, generally applied to the image as a raster operation.

raw [alt. *raw format*] *n.* : A computer file format for pixel images in which red, green, and blue color components for each pixel are entered in successive bytes of the file, starting at the top left corner of the image and proceeding left-to-right and top-to-bottom. The format does not have embedded in it the number of pixels per scanline, which must be communicated separately to read the file, and there is not absolute agreement about the order of the three color components.

ray tracing : An approach to rendering based upon simulating the reflection paths of light among the graphics objects to the viewpoint. Rays for each pixel are typically traced backwards from the viewpoint and among objects until a light source or database boundary is reached.

R-buffering [terminology popularized by Evans & Sutherland Computer Corp.] *n.* : A variant of z-buffering in which occlusion is determined by the true distance from the eye point to each pixel sample point, rather than the distance from a plane through the eye point to each pixel sample point, as computed for convertional z-buffering. R-buffering works with fields of view greater than 180 degrees in a single image, wherein z-buffering fails due to the z-distance becoming zero at the 180-degree extremes. Applications with so wide a field of view in a single image are uncommon, but using true distance also solves a problem of keeping atmospheric haze effects continuous across the boundaries of adjacent images of unequal field-of-view. It is also possible to use z for occlusion and r for haze compution.

real estate distribution : A type of window system input management in which the window containing the cursor is given current input.

realistic rendering : Computer graphics with the objective of producing images that accurately present the lighting, coloring, occlusion, and other aspects of the real world, although not necessarily with databases representing particular real-world objects.

RealityEngine™ : High-performance image generator product of Silicon Graphics, Inc.

real time *adj.* : Responding with apparent continuity and without apparent delay, especially a graphics or other electronic system that provides real-time outputs in response to human inputs. What appears to be continuous and without delay depends upon the application, but real-time graphics generally requires new images 15 times per second with response time less than a quarter of a second. Graphics produced at lower rates or with longer delays are said to be *interactive* rather than *real time*.

recto *n.* : In typesetting, the right-hand page. —Compare VERSO.

reduced instruction set computer : —See RISC.

reference port : The implementation of a software product on a hardware device that establishes the design conventions and serves as a standard for other implementations.

reflectance *n.* : The ratio of the intensity of light reflected from a surface to that incident upon the surface, often expressed as a percentage.

reflectance map : ENVIRONMENTAL MAP.

refraction : The phenomenon of light rays bending when traversing the interface between dissimilar materials. The amount of bend is quantified in terms of the **index of refraction** of the media; the index of refraction is the ratio of the speed of light in a vacuum to that in the medium.

refresh *adj.* : Requiring frequent redrawing, as related to a CRT display with a short-persistence phosphor that must be rescanned continually, the norm for raster displays. The opposite of *storage*. Also, *v.* : to redraw or update.

refresh rate : The rate at which successive frames of a raster display are presented.

registration *n.* : The alignment or degree of alignment of two or more images that overlay, such as the alignment of the color components that add to form a color image.

remote procedure call : —See RPC.

render *v.t.* 1 : To compute an entire scene (as an output array of pixels) from a graphics database. 2 : To convert a graphics primitive into individual pixels.

RenderMan™ [Pixar, Inc.] : High-level graphics package for realistic rendering originated by Pixar, Inc. The interface is offered as a standard.

repaint *v.t.* : To render and display a new version of an image.

Request for Information : —See RFI.

Request for Proposal : —See RFP.

Request for Quotation : —See RFQ.

resize *v.t.* : To change the size of a window.

resolution *n.* 1 : The numbers of pixels in the horizontal and vertical dimensions of a display, such as 1280 x 1024. 2 : The number of elements per unit length available for display or printing by a particular device, such as 300 dots per inch for a printer. 3 : For an optical device or film, the number of alternate light and dark lines per inch that are detectable with prescribed contrast under specified conditions. 4 : For the eye or other image sensor, the number of alternate light and dark lines per unit angle that are detectable with prescribed contrast under specified conditions.

resource *n.* 1 : In graphics, something of limited extent that must be allocated, such as screen space or space in a hardware-limited table. 2 : In management, something needed to do a job; includes people, computers, special equipment, and the like.

resource leveling : The ability of project planning software to schedule tasks in such a way that at no time are predetermined levels of resources exceeded.

retained mode : Graphics processing method in which data are accumulated for later rendering as a group, rather than rendering each data item as it is input. —Compare IMMEDIATE MODE.

retrace *n.* : The portion of a video signal associated with moving a CRT raster scan back to the start of a new scan time (the *horizontal retrace*) or to the start of a new field (*vertical retrace*). The times to accomplish retrace, during which the beam is blanked, are important parameters in a display specification. Since no information is displayed during retrace, graphics hardware is often designed to use these intervals to change color tables and perform other display-related tasks.

retrieval *n.* : In flight simulation graphics, the process of selecting database objects from mass storage according to the present position of the simulated eye point and making them available to a graphics system for rendering.

retroreflectivity *n.* : The fraction of light returned along the line of incidence from a collimated light source for a particular surface and specified angle of incidence.

return on investment : —See ROI.

reverse video : On a two-color display or portion of a two-color display, data in which the roles of the two colors are interchanged from whatever is considered conventional. For example, if characters are usually displayed as bright characters on a dark background, then reverse video would show them as dark on a bright background. This may be used as a means of highlighting a portion of a display, as a key for an attribute not directly displayable (like an unavailable text font), or simply to adapt the display to user preference. : **inverse video.**

revision bar : A thick line in the margin of a document designating a range of text that has been altered from the previous version of the document.

revolute joint *n.* : In a robotic manipulator, a joint that provides a change in the angle between links.

RFI *R-F-I*\\ *n.* 1 : Radio-Frequency Interference; electrical noise at radio frequencies that interferes or potentially interferes with the normal operation of electronic equipment. 2 [government jargon] : Request For Information; a formal request from a U.S. government agency for information, typically concerning the technical feasibility of a contemplated procurement.

RFP *R-F-P*\\ [government jargon] : Request For Proposal; a formal request from a U.S. government agency to provide a detailed implementation description and price for goods and services for which functional specifications are provided.

RFQ *R-F-Q*\\ [government jargon] : Request For Quotation; a request from a U.S. government agency to provide a price quotation for specified goods or services.

RFT *R-F-T*\\ 1 : Regular Full-Time employee. 2 : Ready For Training; in flight simulation, the date when a system is ready for training use.

RGB monitor : Red, Green, Blue *monitor;* a monitor for the display of RGB, as opposed to *composite,* video.

RGB video : Red, Green, Blue *video;* video signals communicated with a separate wire or coaxial cable for each color component. The accompanying synchronization signal may be supplied on a fourth cable or composited on, usually, the green video.

ribbon *n.* : A family of three-dimensional curves, used in graphics for molecular modeling to depict the twisting "backbone" of a molecule.

ribbon cable : Multiple wires held in parallel by a common, usually extruded plastic, insulating material. Usually designed for use in cable assemblies that are rarely disconnected or moved.

RISC *risk*\\ *n.* : Reduced Instruction Set Computer; a style of computer architecture featuring a relatively small set of simple instructions, most of which complete in one cycle or a few cycles.

RLL \R-L-L\ *adj.* : *Run Length Limited*; property of a disk drive controller that compresses data before storage and decompresses the data upon retrieval, using run-length encoding and decoding techniques. This increases the effective capacity of the drive by 50 to 100 percent.

robust *adj.* : Of an algorithm, being able to handle many different types of data including potentially difficult special cases.

Rogers : The noted text *Procedural Elements for Computer Graphics*, by David F. Rogers, McGraw-Hill Book Co., 1985.

ROI \R-O-I\ *n.* 1 : *Return On Investment*; the ratio of monies received from the sale of a product to the money invested in the development and production, often annualized and expressed as a percentage. 2 : *Region Of Interest*; portion of an image identified for further examination or processing in an image-processing system.

roll *n.* : The angular displacement of a vehicle or device about the longitudinal axis, in the plane of the vertical and lateral axes.

ROM \rhymes with *bomb*\ 1 : *Read Only Memory*; digital memory permanently encoded with data at the time of manufacture. —Compare PROM. 2 : *Rough Order-of-Magnitude*; relating to a preliminary estimate cautioned as being an approximation likely to have substantial error.

ROP \rhymes with *top*\ : *Raster Operation*; logical operations (AND, OR, NOT, XOR, etc.) performed on the bit planes of a frame buffer, used to accomplish block moves and the like. Also, *v.t.* : to move data using a ROP.

roping *n.* : An aliasing effect in a graphics image in which a line or thin polygon appears to vary in width, color, or brightness according to a repeating pattern that suggests the braiding of a rope.

Roth diagram [originated by S.D. Roth] : A diagram for ray-tracing models built by constructive solid geometry representing the path of the ray with regions inside and outside the composite model.

round-robin *adj.* : Providing services or resources to multiple requesters or users in simple sequence, starting over with the first after the last is served; as opposed to using a weighted, adaptive, or prioritized method.

Route 128 : Highway circumferential around Boston, MA, noted for its concentration of technology-based companies.

router *n.* 1 : CAD software that determines the physical locations of traces and vias on a printed circuit board to conform to a circuit design and component placement, or the corresponding operations for integrated circuits. 2 : A device that forwards data from one network to another, in accordance with a prescribed protocol.

RPC : Remote Procedure Call; a mechanism allowing a process running on a networked computer to call a subprogram for execution on a different computer on the network.

RS-170A [Recommended Standard] : An IEEE standard for composite video, corresponding to NTSC composite video.

RS-232 [Recommended Standard] : A standard for serial interfaces, commonly used for alphanumeric terminals, modems, and some printers. The precursor to IEEE standard 488 for such interfaces.

rubber-banding : In a drawing environment, sizing an object by fixing one point on it and varying other parameters under the control of a point device. For example, one corner of a rectangle may be fixed, and the opposite corner moved to size the rectangle.

rubber-stamping : Replicating a two-dimensional graphics object by repeatedly dragging and placing the object. Placing the object is done when indicated (typically with a mouse click) by copying the object at its current temporary location.

ruled surface : A surface capable of being generated by sweeping a line through space, or a portion of such a surface.

runarounds _n._ : In typesetting, lines of irregular length used to conform to an irregularly shaped illustration embedded in the text.

run-length encoding : In image processing, a means of compressing binary data by replacing strings of successive ones or zeros by more compact binary code sequences. One mechanism is to give the start address and length of each block of ones on a scanline.

S

sample point : The location relative to the boundaries of a pixel at which the color or z-distance of a pixel is computed for graphics primitives.

sampling *n.* : The process of converting a mathematically described graphics object into a set of discrete values for representation as pixels in a raster image. —Compare POINT SAMPLING, AREA SAMPLING.

sans-serif : The class of typefaces lacking filleted decorations at the edges and ends of strokes of the letters and, usually, having horizontal and vertical strokes of equal thickness. —Compare SERIF.

SAT : *System Aging Test*; a test performed on hardware to determine reliability over time.

saturation *n.* : The property of a color that distinguishes pastels from pure colors.

S-bus : Proposed standard synchronous bus for computer I/O, pioneered by Sun Microsystems. Generally used with small (about 3" x 4") circuit cards.

scalar *adj.* : Characterized by a single number or dimension, as opposed to *vector*, characterized by a set of numbers or multidimensions.

scale *n.* : Size, especially of a two-dimensional graphics representation, often expressed as display units per database unit such as 1/2 inch (on the display or drawing) per foot (of the object represented).

scaling *n.* : The process of changing the scale of a graphics representation.

scan conversion 1 : Converting a graphics primitive into scan lines for rendering and display. 2 : Conversion of a video format using a *scan converter*.

scan converter : A device for converting one video format (specified by frame rate, horizontal and vertical resolutions, and synchronization signal format) into another. Once performed by such expedients as a camera and monitor in a light-tight box, now usually accomplished by the digital manipulation of frame buffered data.

scan design : A method of circuit diagnosis using registers in the design that have a shift mode by which the machine state can be read and set.

scanline [*alt.* scan line, scan-line; also, "scanline" as a noun with "scan-line" as an adjective.] 1 : A complete row of pixels. 2 : A line of a raster display; for example, a horizontal scan of the electron beam on a CRT display. Also, **scanline** *adj.* : related to a scanline.

scanline algorithm : Any rendering algorithm based upon the computation of an image scanline-by-scanline, rather than on an object-by-object or other basis. Scanline algorithms tend to save buffer memory, in that only the information for a single line need be accumulated at one time.

scanner *n.* : A peripheral device for converting a printed image into digital data for subsequent computer processing or display. Typically, a scanner is used to digitize printed documents from which *optical character recognition* software is used to recover the printed text as characters.

schedule *n.* : In management, the dates implied by a plan.

scheduler *n.* : Component of a multitasking software system that determines the order in which tasks, including input and output and user processes, are to be accomplished.

schematic capture : The activity of entering an electronic circuit design interactively into a CAD system using graphic symbols for circuit elements and wires.

Schumacher algorithm : A list priority algorithm that works with a database consisting of clusters of convex polygons with a separating plane tree structure. Used mainly for flight simulation graphics.

SCI 1 : *S*calable *C*oherent *I*nterface; a proposed standard (IEEE P896) interface for system interconnection via bus or more complex network topologies. 2 : *SCI* Systems, Inc., a large (U.S. $1B) company that provides manufacturing services, including surface-mount board assembly, previously named Spacecraft Industries.

scientific visualization *n.* : Data visualization in which the data represent the outcome of a scientific or engineering experiment or calculation, such as data representing the flow of air around a structure being represented as a field of line segments representing samples of flow direction and velocity.

scissoring *n.* : Clipping to the boundaries of the screen using special hardware, especially as part of a calligraphic display system.

SCO *S-C-O*\ : *S*anta *C*ruz *O*peration; Santa Cruz, CA, company providing UNIX-compatible software for personal computers and workstations.

scotopic *adj.* : Related to achromatic vision in dim light, sensed by rods in the retina of the eye. —Compare PHOTOPIC.

screen coordinates : The coordinate system associated with the pixels on the display device.

screen door transparency : A graphics effect produced by rendering only a patterned subset of the pixels for an object so that otherwise-occluded objects will be partially visible. For example, a 50 percent transparency effect can be achieved by writing only the pixels of an object corresponding to a checkerboard pattern, with the "holes" in the pattern allowing those pixels from another object to appear alternately.

screen extent : The minimum coordinate-axis-aligned rectangle enclosing a line segment or other two-dimensional graphics object.

screen size : The maximum diagonal measure of the image-producing area of a display.

scribe *n.* : In integrated circuit design, the space allowed at the periphery of a layout to allow for the mechanical separation of the silicon wafer into dice.

scroll bars : Rectangular regions bordering a window that may be selected to control scrolling of the contents of the window. The portion of the scroll bar selected usually determines the scrolling characteristics such as the direction and rate.

scrolling *n.* : Moving an image horizontally or vertically in a fixed window, usually by performing a block move of much of the data within the window and adding new data along one edge.

scroll rate : The rate at which an image can be moved within a window, especially, the rate (in characters per second) at which text can be added to a window that is scrolling vertically.

SCS *S-C-S*\ : *S*canning and *C*onversion *S*ystem; an integrated system for converting hand-drafted drawings to raster images, interactively modifying them, and preparing new hard-copy output.

SCSI *scuzzy*\ : *S*mall *C*omputer *S*ystem *I*nterface; a medium-speed byte-wide I/O bus for peripherals, especially disk storage devices.

sculptured surface : A free-form surface.

SDRC *S-D-R-C*\ : *S*tructural *D*ynamics *R*esearch *C*o.; Ohio company producing MCAD tools.

SECAM *see-cam*\ : *S*ysteme *E*lectronique *C*ouleur *A*vec *M*emoire; television standard used principally in France and the former USSR. Video for SECAM transmission is typically generated and recorded in PAL format, and is encoded into SECAM only immediately prior to transmission.

section plane : A plane defined in the coordinate system of a modeled object so that the object may be clipped to provide a cut-away view.

section space : A volume defined by a collection of planes in world coordinates that serves to clip subsequently rendered objects; each plane defining the volume has an inclusive and exclusive side that contributes to the definition of the volume through the specification of a set of Boolean rules.

seed fill : Algorithm for coloring the interior of a connected two-dimensional region defined by a bit-mapped boundary in which pixels nearest a starting point are colored in succession.

segment *n.* 1 : An individual polynomial curve in an assembly of such curves forming a spline curve. 2 : A line segment. 3 : In the GKS standard, a collection of attributes and primitives. [These are called *structures* in PHIGS.] 4 : A block of virtual memory that is mapped in the first level of a memory management unit. 5. Any block of memory that serves an allocation function, such as a *data segment* or a *program segment.*

selective erase : Erasing (or overwriting with the background color) specified graphics objects without rewriting or otherwise affecting the remainder of the image.

selector *n.* : An electronic circuit having more than one data input and one data output, plus a control signal that selects which data input will be transferred to the output.

self-similarity : A property of a graphics or natural object in which a portion of the object is a miniature version of the whole. If the portion is not an exact replica of the whole but shares certain average characteristics, as is the case with natural objects, then the object has **statistical self-similarity.** An example is a tree branch where smaller branches bear similarity to the whole branch. In graphics, the concept is useful in the modeling of natural objects including plant life, terrain, and clouds. —See also, FRACTAL.

separating plane tree : An auxiliary data structure comprising mathematical planes between the graphics objects in a database designed to facilitate placing the objects in occlusion priority order; mainly used for flight simulator graphics.

serialization *n.* : Ensuring that data sent from a source to a destination for processing is processed in the order in which it was sent.

serif *adj.* : Related to the class of typefaces having small filleted decorations at the edges and ends of strokes of the letters and, usually, having horizontal strokes thinner than vertical. —Compare

SANS-SERIF. Also, *n.* : one of the small filleted horizontal strokes in a serif typeface.

A serif typeface   A sans-serif typeface

server *n.* 1 : A computer shared over a network, usually to provide common storage or compute resources. 2 : A type of window management software system, not necessarily in remote hardware, in which the mechanization is not embedded in the operating system kernel.

server user : A graphics system user running on the same machine as the window server that elects to perform all accesses to graphics devices directly through the window server via a window interface.

SGI : Silicon Graphics, Inc.; a major vendor of three-dimensional graphics workstations, especially medium- and high-performance systems.

shader *n.* : The portion of a graphics rendering system that computes the effects of illumination upon visible surfaces.

shades of gray 1 : Steps of intensity available in a graphics or display system. 2 : Steps of intensity in which successive steps are in a ratio equal to the square root of two. The number of such steps that a display system can produce being taken as a measure of performance. —See also, GRAY SCALE.

shading *n.* 1 : The visual effects of light sources upon an object, as computed in a graphics system. In simple models only effects independent of other objects are included so that surface properties and self-shadowing are taken into account, but not secondary reflections or shadows from other objects. More complex models, such as those used for ray tracing and radiosity calculations, take nearly all of the subtleties into account. —See also, GOURAUD SHADING, PHONG SHADING. 2 : A defect in a display device resulting in an unintended brightness gradient over a large portion of the display.

shading model : The algorithm used to compute the effects of light upon a surface in a particular graphics system : an illumination model.

shadow map : An array of depth values created from the viewpoint of a point light source giving the distance to the first surface encountered for the direction corresponding to each array address. The array is subsequently used, with transformations from the viewpoint of a scene being rendered, to test if points on object surfaces are in shadow.

shadow mask : A perforated metal plate positioned between the electron guns and the phosphor dots of a color cathode ray tube, so that each hole aligns the beams from the three-color electron guns with their corresponding phosphor color dots.

shadow register : An Advanced Micro Devices circuit construction that allows the synchronous sampling of data and the asynchronous shifting out of diagnostic information.

Shapes : A Sun Microsystems graphics package for two-dimensional applications; the platform upon which Sun's X11/NeWS is implemented.

sharpening *n.* : An image-processing operation that enhances edges and details.

shear *adj.* : Relating to a coordinate transformation in which the angles between axes are changed.

shoe box : A shoe box–sized electronic package usually containing disk and cartridge tape units for a workstation that does not accept these units internally.

shutter glasses *pl. n.* : a device worn like eyeglasses for stereo viewing of graphics imagery, and which alternately opens and blocks vision of the left and right eyes in synchronism with a display that presents the corresponding view. The glasses are typically implemented with electronically controlled liquid-crystal shutters alternating at 120 Hz.

siccade *n.* : Long-range motion of the eye when repositioning from one object to another. Visual input is suppressed during and shortly after a siccade, a property used in eye-tracked displays to provide for repositioning to the new direction of view.

SIF : *S*imulator *I*nterchange *F*ormat, U.S. government–sponsored format for exchanging simulation database information.

SIGGRAPH *sig-graph*\ 1 : The ACM's *S*pecial *I*nterest *G*roup for *Graph*ics, the major professional group for graphics professionals. 2 : An annual conference for graphics professionals, traditionally held in the U.S. in late July or early August, having a unique status of prestige and importance in the profession.

signal-to-noise ratio : —See SNR.

signature analysis : A means of testing digital circuits in which a computed function of the expected outputs is compared with an expected value of the precomputed function. The functions shorten the pattern results saved in storage (analogous to a parity check).

silhouette edge : An edge of a graphics object that when projected separates pixels of the object from those of the rest of the image. For convex polyhedra having outward-facing surface normals, the silhouette edges lie between adjacent front-facing and back-facing polygons. Silhouette edges are treated as special cases by some antialiasing algorithms.

Silicon Graphics, Inc. : —See SGI.

Silicon Valley [The name derives from the widespread use of silicon-based integrated circuit technology; there is no actual geographic feature having the name.] : A portion of the Santa Clara Valley (starting approximately 50 miles south of San Francisco) including the cities of Palo Alto, Mountain View, Sunnyvale, Santa Clara, Cupertino, and San Jose, among others, noted as having the headquarters of many technology-based companies.

simulation *n.* 1 : Testing or analysis of an algorithm, circuit, or system by constructing a version in software and applying test cases to it. Simulation may be applied hierarchically so that, for example, a high-level simulation embodies a multiplier in a circuit by a multiply instruction in a high-level language and a low-level simulation used models of the gates forming the multiplier used in the circuit. Some use the terms *simulation* and emulation to distinguish between the two levels, but there is no strong consensus as to which term is to be used for which level. 2 : Mechanization of a function by other than the original or traditional means, such as to perform a function in software that is alternatively implemented in hardware. 3 : FLIGHT SIMULATION or other vehicle simulation, typically performed for training or analysis.

sink *n.* : In the layout of a published page, extra white space at the top of each page to emphasize the body of text.

6-D.O.F. [*six doff*] *adj.* : Having six degrees of freedom of motion, namely, three axes of translation and three angles of rotation.

skew transform : A geometric transformation that alters the angle between the axes, for example, a transform that changes rectangles to parallelograms.

slew rate : The rate at which a system pans through an image file, usually measured in the database units per second.

slice *v.t.* : To apply section-plane clipping to a model.

Small Computer System Interface : —See SCSI.

SMD \S-M-D\ *n.* 1 : Storage Module Drive; a type of fast hard-disk drive. Also, *adj.* : being of the SMD type. Sometimes used redundantly <an SMD drive>. 2 : Surface Mount Device; an electronic component designed to be mounted on a circuit board without drilling holes for the leads.

smooth shading : The process of rendering graphics imagery having continuous variations of tones over a region. —Compare FLAT SHADING, GOURAUD SHADING.

SMPTE *simpty*\ : Society of Motion Picture and Television Engineers.

SMT *S-M-T*\ *n.* : Surface Mount Technology; the technology by which printed circuit board assemblies are manufactured without soldering component leads through holes in the boards. Components are soldered to surface pads instead. The advantages are higher circuit density, and in some cases, reduced component costs and superior electrical characteristics.

snap *v.t.* : In a CAD system, to automatically reposition the cursor to the nearest point on a line or its extension, to the midpoint of a line, or to an intersection of two lines. —Compare GRAVITY.

Snell's law : The law governing the refraction of light, the sine of the incident angle being equal to the refractive index of the material times the sine of the refracted angle. A law vital to the rendering of ray-traced glass spheres that are so popular in computer graphics.

snow *n.* : The displayed image of noise on a video signal.

SNR : Signal-to-Noise Ratio; in image processing, the ratio of energy in the desired image to that of an undesired noise component. The ratio is usually expressed in decibels.

soft copy 1 : A copy of digital data on floppy disk, tape, or other digital recording media. 2 [uncommon] : Data output to a CRT or other display. —Compare HARD COPY.

soft return : In word processing, a carriage return inserted automatically by the software to wrap text to the next line, and automatically repositioned as required by editing of the text.

SOIC *S-O-I-C*\ : Small-Outline Integrated Circuit; the packages used for surface mounting.

SOJ *S-O-J*\ : Small-Outline J-lead; an integrated circuit package.

solids modeling : Modeling using constructive solid geometry techniques.

solid texture : A texture function defined in three-dimensional space for texturing objects so they will appear carved out of a material having an internal pattern, such as wood or stone.

sonic tablet : A digitizing tablet in which the position of the stylus is determined by timing the travel of sound pulses emitted by the stylus to two or more microphones in fixed positions. Stripmicrophones, which are sensitive over a linear region, are conventionally used along two edges of a two-dimensional tablet, with a third added vertically for three dimensions.

SpaceBall™ : Control device for supplying position and orientation data to a computer through manipulation of an instrumented ball attached to an arm support.

spaghetti model : Storage of spatial data, especially the outlines of features on a map, as a string of x-y coordinates without other spatial relationship data.

span *n.* 1 : A group of pixels, usually along a scanline, that are processed concurrently by hardware in a graphics accelerator. 2 : The pixels along a scanline between edges of a triangle or convex polygon.

SPARC™ *spark*\\ [Sun Microsystems, Inc.] *n.* : *S*calable *P*rocessor *Arc*hitecture, Sun Microsystems' RISC architecture, embodied in several different chip technologies. The basis of the Sun-4 product line, and available as components for general use. Also, *adj.* : of or related to the SPARC.

spatial *adj.* : Varying in space, for example, as a function of the Cartesian coordinates.

SPEC Benchmark Suite : *S*ystem *P*erformance *E*valuation *C*ooperative Benchmark Suite; a set of software for evaluating different aspects of computer system performance, agreed to by a group of companies as representing industry-standard benchmarks.

special effect : In flight simulation graphics, a visual effect, such as that of a fire burning, achieved by substitution of one or more database objects with alternate versions in a predetermined sequence.

speckle *n.* : A nonadditive noise effect in images formed by monochromatic (usually laser) light reflected from surfaces having roughness on the same order as the wavelength of light, thereby producing local interference patterns. A special partially translucent surface can be used to minimize the effect on laser projection screens and the like.

spectrophotometer *n.* : A device capable of measuring light intensities in different spectral regions, in particular for determining the CIE coordinates of a color. A scanning spectrophotometer measures light intensities in narrow bands, scanning the spectrum, from which CIE coordinates are computed by numerical integration.

specular reflection : The reflection from a shiny or mirrorlike surface.

sphere primitive : A graphics primitive sought by molecular modeling users to represent atoms; generally implies an orthographic rendering.

spherical product surface : A surface generated from two curves with each curve having x and y components defined by parametric equations, where the x component of the surface is the product of the x equations of the two curves, the y component of the surface is the product of the x equation of the first curve and y equation of the second curve, and the z component of the surface is the x equation of the first curve. The spherical product surface generated from two circles is a sphere.

splat [UNIX *slang*] *n.* : The pound sign, "#"

spline curve : A continuous curve composed of adjacent polynomial segments. —See also JOINT, KNOT.

Spox : Name of the Spectron operating system for TI's TMS320C30 DSP chip.

spraying *n.* : A feature of a digital paint system mimicking the action of a spray gun by painting a fine pattern of pixels.

sprite *n.* : A raster marker, usually in the context of a movable pattern used in video game graphics.

squashing *n.* : —See STRETCHING.

SSI \S-S-I\ : Small Scale Integration; integrated circuits having the lowest level of complexity, roughly in the range of 2 to 20 gates or the equivalent.

staircasing *n.* : An aliasing effect in a graphics image in which a line or edge of a polygon appears jagged, like the profile of a staircase, rather than straight.

standalone *adj.* : Not connected to a network, or operating as if not connected to a network.

standard cell : In integrated circuit technology, a design methodology using predesigned circuit patterns having rectangular boundaries with one of the boundary dimensions constant for the design. The cells are arranged in uniform-width columns for convenience in automatically routing the interconnections.

statefull *adj.* : Related to software or hardware that retains stored parameters for use in processing subsequent data.

stateless *adj.* : Related to software or hardware that retains no data for subsequent processing, and for which all parameters must be input with associated data. For example, a stateless routine to draw triangles would not remember the current color or illumination parameter, and would require that such parameters be supplied along with each set of triangle vertices.

Stellar Computer, Inc. : Newton, MA, company producing the Stellar Graphics Supercomputer, an applications accelerator that as a graphics machine, claims 150K shaded triangles or 600K three-dimensional vectors per second. Now defunct.

stencil *adj.* : Related to a mode of writing into a frame buffer, generally with hardware support, in which the ones of incoming bit patterns are translated to a predetermined color and corresponding pixels in the frame buffer are overwritten. The pixels corresponding to the zeros of the incoming pattern are left untouched <stencil mode>.

stereo *n.* : True three-dimensional viewing achieved in computer graphics by supplying separately computed images for each eye. A simple method is to compute two images side-by-side on a CRT display and view them through an optical combining device. An alternative is to provide a liquid-crystal-based plate assembly in front of a CRT, the plate assembly reverses the polarization of the light on successive frames of the display so that suitably synchronized images appear in stereo to a user wearing glasses having left and right lenses each admitting one of the two polarizations. Yet another method equips the viewer with glasses having liquid-crystal shutters synchronized to the successive left-right images on the display.

Stereographics, Inc. : Major supplier of stereo equipment for computer graphics displays; located in San Rafael, CA.

stilb *n.* : A unit of luminance equal to 0.0001 nit.

stipple *n.* 1 : A pattern of dots or short dashes. 2 : In the X Window System, a bit map of a tile that is to be used as a stencil when filling a region with the foreground color. Also, *v.t.* : to fill a region with a stipple.

stochastic sampling : A technique for antialiasing in which a sequence of images are computed, each computed using point sampling for each pixel but with the sample points varying from image to image. The antialiased image is computed as the average of the corresponding pixels from the sequence of images, so that only the current image and the sum of the previous images need be stored concurrently. The locations of the sample points may be chosen randomly or (in contradiction to the name) according to a regular grid for computational convenience. (Nonregular locations of sample points generally produces more effective antialiasing for a given number of samples, however.)

storage tube : —See DVST.

streaking *n.* : A display or computation error in which portions of displayed objects extend horizontally outside of their normal boundaries.

stretching *n.* : Deforming a graphic model by increasing the scaling in one direction and decreasing the scaling in orthogonal directions, mimicking the stretching of a physical object. In animation, stretching is sometimes used, for example, in the direction of motion to emphasize speed. The opposite deformation, decreasing the scale in one direction and increasing in the others is **squashing.**

string device : In GKS, an input device, such as a keyboard, that supplies a string of characters.

strip *n.* : A mesh of, usually, triangles or quads that is one primitive wide.

Triangle Strip

stroke device : In GKS, an input device, such as a digitizing tablet, providing a sequence of points to which a normalizing transformation is applied.

stroke display : CALLIGRAPHIC DISPLAY.

stroker [*slang*] *n.* : CALLIGRAPHIC DISPLAY.

stroke text : Text drawn using lines, usually to facilitate transformation operations on the text, not necessarily using a calligraphic display, however.

strong *adj.* : Being both relatively high in color saturation and moderate in color value.

structure text *n.* : Text subject to a full transformation pipeline so as to be scaled, rotated, put in perspective, etc.: —See ANNOTATION TEXT.

style *n.* 1 : An attribute of a line corresponding to a modulation to the intensity or opacity of a line, generally tied to the origin of the line but not subject to perspective, as a dotted or dashed line. 2 : TYPE STYLE.

stylus *n.* 1 : The penlike entry instrument used with a graphics tablet. 2 : One of an array of fine metal conductors used to transfer charge to the media in an electrostatic plotter.

subatomic primitive *n.* : A graphics primitive used as an intermediary in rendering, such as a primitive that specifies rendering a scanline according to certain parameters.

subdivision *n.* : Breaking a curve or surface into smaller pieces, usually recursively. Also, **subdivide** *v.t.* : to accomplish subdivision.

subpixel : A subdivision of the area represented by a pixel, usually for the purpose of performing antialiasing by using finer-grained calculations that are ultimately summed to obtain the color component values associated with the whole pixel.

subpixel addressability : —See ADDRESSABILITY.

subscript *n.* : Characters printed below the normal baseline for a line of type and usually reduced in size. Also, *v.t.* : to typeset in subscript; *adj.* : below the baseline.

subtractive color model : The color model appropriate to mixing inks and paints, where the pigments absorb some colors of incident light and reflect others. The primaries used are cyan, magenta, and yellow. —See also, CMYK.

succolarity [coined by B. Mandelbrot, from Latin sub + *percolare,* to almost flow through. c. 1977] *n.* : The property of a fractal having filaments that nearly fill space, i.e., without leaving empty regions. **Nonlacunar** seems to be preferred to the potential adjective form **succolar**. —Compare LACUNARITY.

Sun-3™ : Family of Sun Microsystems' workstation products based upon the Motorola 680x0 microprocessors.

Sun-4™ : Family of Sun Microsystems' workstation products based upon the SPARC processors.

Sun Microsystems, Inc. [Andreas Bechtolshiem called his workstation project at Stanford "SUN" as an abbreviation for Stanford University Network; this work was key to the company's first product and inspired the company name] : Mountain View, CA, major vendor of UNIX workstations.

superblack *n.* : In a video signal, a voltage level below that used for normal black image video, used for color keying. Also, *adj.* : having a level corresponding to superblack.

superblock *n.* : In UNIX, a data structure that holds the basic parameters of the file system.

supercase *n.* : In typesetting, a set of characters, usually special symbols, that are neither upper nor lower case and are accessed by a reserved *supershift* code. Also, *adj.* : being in the supercase character set.

supercomputer *n.* : A computer that has high storage capacity and, especially, high processing speed relative to whatever is common for minicomputers and workstations. A factor of, very roughly, 25 in the speed category is the starting point.

superconic *n.* : Generalization of a conic curve in which the trigonometric terms in the formula for the curve are raised to an arbitrary power that controls the smoothness of the curve.

superimpose *v.t.* : To place an image including transparent or partially transparent regions on top of another image; such as to superimpose text on video : to overlay.

superquadric *n.* : A generalization of quadric surfaces formed as the *spherical product surface* of two *superconics*. Includes, for example, a **superellipsoid,** in which the smoothness of the surface may be adjusted from a conventional ellipsoidal shape to a rectangular box shape. The surfaces may be converted to an implicit form for ray tracing.

superred, supergreen, superblue *n.* : The mathematically defined primaries of the CIE color space. These primaries cannot be realized as physical colors because they would require the equivalent of negative intensities of spectral color components, but they serve as useful abstractions by which any real color can be specified as having components of these three **super primaries.**

supersampling *n.* : Reducing aliasing and subpixel occlusion errors by computing multiple sample points within a pixel, and assigning the appropriately weighted average of thc subpixel values to the pixel : OVERSAMPLING. Also, **supersample** *v.i.* : to antialias by supersampling.

superscalar *adj.* : Capable of executing more than one operation concurrently as part of a single instruction, such as a RISC processor having instructions for performing multiply and add operations in parallel. —See also, MICROPARALLELISM.

superscript *n.* : Characters printed above the normal baseline for a line of type and usually reduced in size. Also, *v.t.* : to typeset in superscript; *adj.* : above the baseline.

supershift *adj.* : Initiating the use of supercase.

superuser *n.* 1 : A system or network user having access to certain data ordinarily protected from modification, typically that required for system or network administration. 2 : A mode of operation on an individual workstation, provided to help prevent accidental modification of configuration files.

Super VGA : —See VGA.

Super VHS™ : —See VHS.

superwhite *n.* : High-intensity white achieved by a special input to a video digital-to-analog converter that results in an output voltage typically 10 percent greater than obtainable from the usual data inputs. The objective is to provide a cursor that is visible against the white produced from image data. Also, *adj.* : being superwhite.

surface mapping : —See MAP.

surface normal : A unit vector defined at each point on the surface of a graphics object, usually perpendicular to the plane tangent to the surface at that point. The surface normal may be defined differently from that implied by the surface geometry in order to achieve a particular illumination effect, such as *bump mapping* or to minimize apparent faceting for curved-surface approximations. Surface normals may be multiply defined at edges where there are discontinuities, such as the circular edges of a cylinder.

surface of revolution : A three-dimensional surface that can be generated by sweeping a planar curve around a central axis.

Sutherland-Hodgman algorithm : Algorithm for clipping a polygon to a convex clipping region, in which the input polygon is clipped against a region edge, with the output of that operation supplied to the next region edge, repeating the process until all of the region edges have been applied. Referred to as *reentrant polygon clipping*.

S-VHS™ : —See VHS.

swash character *n.* : In a typeface, an alternate character having a curved flourish that extends over or under adjacent characters.

sweeping *n.* : Generating a surface implicitly by moving a curve over a trajectory. Also, **sweep** *v.t.* : to produce by sweeping.

swimming *n.* : A stability defect in a video image in which portions of the image move in an undulating pattern.

swizzle *v.t.* : To reverse the left-to-right order of bits in a byte, usually to convert data for a processor having a different convention of bit ordering.

symbolic link : In a computer file system, a means of automatically routing data to a file indirectly, as specified by the link, rather than directly.

synchronous *adj.* : Having events linked so as to establish them in a fixed relationship in time, especially electronic circuitry in which the logic events are keyed to a periodic clock signal.

syntactic sugar : A change in computer language syntax or the format of a subprogram call just to improve comprehension of the function performed; terminology originated by LISP programmers, who find the notion peculiar.

T

tablet *n.* : A digitizer.

tactile feedback *n.* : Stimulation of the sense of touch as a means of communicating information from an electronic system to a user. Most often *tactile feedback* refers to the use of small motions or vibrations to stimulate the skin, whereas *force feedback* refers to applied external forces sensed by the resistance to muscle-induced pressure or motion.

tactor *n.* : An element, usually in an array of like elements, that provides stimulus for the sense of touch.

TARGA : —See TGA.

task *n.* : In project management, an element of an activity network comprising a description of work to be done, the resources required, the end product, and the estimated duration of the task.

TCP/IP *T-C-P-I-P*\\ : Transmission Control Protocol/*I*nternetwork Protocol; a transport-level network protocol developed for ARPANET and, subsequently, widely used as a standard.

teapot : A time-honored graphics database, originated by Martin Newell, used to develop, test, and demonstrate graphics algorithms. The surfaces have different curvatures, so it provides a reasonably comprehensive test case. The original teapot from which the database was digitized now resides in the Computer Museum in Boston.

Technical Office Protocol : —See TOP.

telecommuting *n.* : Working at home or at a location other than the primary work site of an organization, through the use of computers and communication technology so as to avoid traveling to the site.

teleconference *n.* : A conference involving participants at remote locations, facilitated with audio and video communication links.

teleconferencing *n.* : Holding a conference among parties at two or more locations through the use of closed-circuit video transmissions. The video is typically digitally compressed and restored to minimize the bandwidth and associated costs of transmission.

teledildonics *n.* : Sexual activity accomplished with communications between remote devices used by the participants; much more a concept than an actuality at present : CYBERSEX.

teleoperation *n.* : Human remote control of a vehicle, tool, or other instrument based upon communicating sensory inputs from the remote location to the human and control actions back to the instrument, the object being to simulate presence at the site.

telepresence *n.* : The experience of a human interacting with a remote environment as if the person were present in that remote location, usually through use of communication to a robotic device having video cameras and manipulators at the remote location.

telerobotics *n.* : Operation of a robot under remote control, usually by a human operator and often with use of long-distance communication links.

teletex *n.* : Transmission of encoded text as a hidden part of a broadcast video signal, for selective decoding and display by the receiving equipment. —Compare VIDEOTEX.

template matching : In image processing, detection of features in an image by convolving an array (the template) embodying the feature with the image and thresholding the result.

temporal *adj.* : Varying in time. In graphics and image processing, the common temporal reference is to successive frames of an animated or video image. —Compare SPATIAL.

tension *n.* : The relative amount of curvature near the control points of a curve of surface; analogous to the tension applied to a rope constrained by pulleys.

teraflop [coined by James Kajiya in discussions of the computational requirements for ray tracing] *n.* : one trillion (10^{12}) floating point operations.

tessellate *v.t.* : To subdivide a surface into a collection of smaller figures; for example, to approximate a curved surface by triangles.

test suite : Series of inputs and expected results applied to test a software product.

test vector : A pattern of ones and zeros applied to a circuit to produce an output for comparison to a precomputed expected result.

Texas Instruments, Inc. : Dallas, TX, company producing semiconductor products and electronic systems, notably signal- processing chips (the TMS320Cx0 series) and graphics processor chips (the TMS340x0 series).

texel [apparently from *tex*ture *el*ements] *n.* : A stored solid texture pattern composed of elements including surface and lighting model data.

text *n.* : Character data, such as encoded letters, numbers, and punctuation marks, as opposed to images or other data.

textual *adj.* : Composed entirely of text, without images or other data.

texture *n.* : A modulation of color, intensity, surface normal, transparency, or other surface property applied to the surface of a graphics object in such a way that the pattern appears attached to the surface as the viewpoint and perspective varies. —Compare PATTERN. Also, *v.t.* : to apply a texture. —See also, SOLID TEXTURE, BUMP MAPPING, MAP.

texture mapping : —See MAP.

TEX™ *teck* or, according to the originator, *tecchhh* with the *ch* sound as in Scottish *loch* or German *ach*\ [originated by Donald Knuth, from Greek lúx meaning *art* and *technology*] [American Mathematical Society] : Comprehensive typesetting software package especially well-suited to presenting mathematical notation.

TGA \from Truevison's TARGA frame buffer products\ : File format for color images. —Compare VST.

thermal dye transfer printing : A type of high-resolution color technology used in color printers and copiers, based upon selective transfer of dyes from a dye-bearing media to paper.

3-D graphics : Graphics derived from a three-dimensional database, requiring projection to two dimensions for screen display.

3-D picking : —See PICKING.

three-dimensional sound [alt. 3-D sound] *n.* : reproduced or synthesized sound intended to give the impression of the sound sources coming from a direction in space including front-and-back and above-and-below cues, as distinguished from stereo sound providing only left-and-right directionality. The additional cueing beyond that afforded by stereo sound is provided by simulating phase and frequency variations associated with the orientation of the head and ears with respect to the sound source.

thresholding *n.* : In image processing, selection of one of two algorithms for processing a pixel based upon comparison of the pixel value, or a computation on neighboring pixels, to a constant. A simple case is outputting black or white depending upon whether the pixel value is above or below a certain gray level.

thumbwheel *n.* : An input device having the edge of a wheel-like knob exposed through a slot in a panel. The knob is rotated with the thumb against the exposed edge.

TI : Texas Instruments, Inc.

TIFF : [*Tagged Image File Format, tiff*] *n.* : One of a number of formats for storing compressed digital images. Originated in the context of images scanned in for incorporation into a document. **TIFF-P** is a variation for 8-bit indexed color, and is similar to GIF. **TIFF-R** is an extension for 24-bit true-color imagery.

TIGA-340™ [Texas Instruments] : *Texas Instrument Graphics Architecture*; graphics hardware interface standard originated for TI's TMS340 graphics processor chips.

tile *v.t.* : To cover a plane with nonoverlapping polygons or other contiguous geometric objects.

tiled windows : Windows that by the design of the window system are not allowed to overlap. Most contemporary window systems allow overlapping windows.

time of day : In flight simulation graphics, the aspects of a simulation related to the position of the sun and day or night illumination levels.

token *n.* : A bit sequence used as an identifying pattern of bits, rather than as a representation of a binary number.

toolkit *n.* 1 : Utility software for window system applications programming used to facilitate implementation of a user interface. 2 : In general, any utility package used to facilitate an implementalion.

TOP : *Technical Office Protocol*; computer network standards for the automated office environment.

topological model : Storage of spatial data, especially the outlines of geographic map features, in which relationships to adjacent lines and polygons are explicitly recorded.

topology *n.* : The set of geometric properties related to connectivity rather than to specific shape or size. **Network topology** concerns the means by which nodes are interconnected, for example, in a ring or star arrangement. Also, *adj.* : **topological;** *adv.* : **topologically.**

torus *n.* : A doughnut-shaped surface, defined as that swept by a circle rotated around a coplanar nonintersecting line. *pl.* **tori.** Also, **toroidal** *adj.* : having the topological properties of a torus.

touchscreen [*alt.* touch screen] : A display surface equipped to detect and position the point of contact of a fingertip on the surface. The positioning serves as input to, for example, select an item from a menu displayed behind the surface. Certain touchscreens use optical sensors so that only close proximity to the screen, rather than actual contact, is required.

trace *n.* : A narrow metal strip serving as a wire on a printed circuit board.

track ball [*alt.* trackball; *unc. alt.* tracker ball] : A pointing device transmitting horizontal and vertical relative position changes in response to the user rotating a stationary caged ball by friction against the hand.

tracker *n.* : A device for determining the position or the position and angular orientation of an object in space. Trackers operate with various mechanisms, including mechanical connection, sensing of continuous and pulsed magnetic fields, infrared and visible optics, and acoustic sensing. For virtual reality applications head, body, and wand motions are typically tracked over ranges from a few feet to a few tens of feet.

tracking *n.* : In typesetting, control of the average spacing between letters and the average spacing between words to determine the density of the text.

tracking cross : A displayed symbol created to support a light pen and moved with the light pen, so that the light pen will have a detectable object in otherwise blank portions of the screen. One alternative is to provide a dark blue background, rather than a black background, so that a blue-sensitive pen will always have detectable video.

trajectory *n.* 1 : The path of a moving object, or a point on a moving object, through space 2 : The path followed by a robotic manipulator in reaching a destination position.

translation : Relocation of a graphics object by a combination of motions parallel to the coordinate axes; a transformation independent of rotation or scaling.

translucent *adj.* : Partially transparent with some additional blurring of the partially obscured image. Also, **translucency** *n.* : the visual effect of being translucent.

Transmission Control Protocol/Internetwork Protocol : —See TCP/IP.

transparency *n.* : The visual effect of an object partially obscuring what is behind it. The effects may be rendered via an analytical calculation as part of a *ray tracing* approach, or by weighted averaging with a *painter's algorithm* approach. Note that there are two physical phenomena associated with transparency. In one case, such as being partially obscured by smoke or fog, a fraction of the color of the obscured object(s) is added to a fraction of the color of the obscuring object. In the other case, as with a colored filter or a colored glass object, the spectral components of the partially obscured object are selectively reduced. Also, **transparent** *adj.* : partially obscuring. —See also, SCREEN DOOR TRANSPARENCY.

transparent *n.* : Automatically invoked hardware or software mechanisms used so that a user is not, and need not, be aware of specific methods used. For example, acceleration hardware that is used automatically whenever it is plugged into a system is transparent.

transport *n.* 1 : In the OSI model of networking, the layer of services providing reliable network-independent end-to-end communications over the network. The lower layers provide technology-dependent network services. 2 : In a computer system, a set of bus interface hardware designed for reuse in each of the different subsystems on the bus.

transport delay : In flight simulation, the time from the initiation of a control motion until the completion of the first field of video having an image updated to reflect the corresponding change in the computed eyepoint position.

traversal *n.* : The process of sequentially referencing the elements of a display list, processing them as required, and transmitting selected graphics commands and data to hardware for display. **Software traversal** : Traversal performed by software operating on the host processor. **Hardware traversal** : Traversal performed by specialized graphics hardware. **Multiprocessor traversal** : Traversal performed by a processor in a multiprocessing system, separate from the processor hosting the graphics application originating the data. Also, **traverse** *v.t.* : to carry out traversal.

triangulate *v.t.* : To subdivide a polygon into triangles to simplify rendering.

triboluminescence *n.* : Light generated by friction. Sometimes the source of a problem in electrostatic printing technology when friction between toner and paper produced unwanted light.

trigger *n.* : In GKS, an input device used by an operator to signal an event. For example, a mouse button used to initiate capture of the current cursor position.

trim curve : A curve used to bound a surface.

Trinitron™ [Sony Corp.] : A type of color cathode ray tube in which the electron guns are arranged in-line, vertical wires are used instead of a shadow mask, and phosphors are arrayed in vertical stripes on the face plate. The advantages are brighter colors and improved vertical resolution, but the mask is not self-supporting, which limits the size of the display.

tristimulus values : The coordinates of a color represented in the CIE color space, XYZ.

true color 1 : Color for graphics in which the entire color space available to the device is represented by digital samples, most typically by storing values for the red, green, and blue components. The alternative representation is *indexed color*. 2 : [*uncommon*] Representation of the entire visible color space.

TSR : *T*erminate and *S*tay *R*esident; an MS-DOS program, a portion of which stays memory-resident to facilitate recall of the program or use of it in conjunction with another program, thereby implementing a primitive form of multitasking.

TTY \ *T-T-Y*\ [a *telety*pe terminal] *adj*. : Providing a basic set of alphanumeric and control characters, without graphics <a TTY emulation window>.

turnkey system : A completely integrated system, including computer, application software, and peripherals, supplied to a customer as a package.

tweening [*slang*] *n.* : INBETWEENING.

two-and-a-half dimensional graphics : Two-dimensional graphics in which objects are assigned an occlusion priority to determine how they overlap. Most two-dimensional graphics are actually of this sort.

2-D graphics : Graphics in which the source databases are two-dimensional, for example, electrical computer-aided design, desktop publishing graphics, or business graphics. More examples of 2-D graphics are pie charts, bar graphs, etc.

2-D picking : —See PICKING.

typeface *n.* : A design for a family of letters, numbers, and other characters used in publishing. —See FONT.

type style *n.* : One of the style variations of a typeface, such as a bold or italic version.

U

ULSI \ *U-L-S-I*\ : *U*ltra *L*arge *S*cale *I*ntegration; the class of integrated circuit devices having a complexity of roughly 200,000 to 20,000,000 gates, or the equivalent. [Some sources extend the upper boundary to a billion gates or more.]

U-matic™ [Sony] : A format for recording television video on 3/4-inch tape cassettes, especially in industrial use, now facing obsolescence.

UNIBUS™ [trademark, DEC] : A medium-speed computer I/O bus originated by DEC.

uniform *adj* : Having equally spaced subdivisions, as a uniform spline in which the knots are equally spaced. Unequally spaced subdivisions are *nonuniform*.

union *n.* : In constructive solid geometry, the region in three-dimensional space within either of two or more specified solid objects. —Compare INTERSECTION.

UNIX™ [Originated by K. Thompson and D. Ritchie; the name parodied an early operating system named *Multics* that attempted to do many things, whereas *UNIX* sought to do one thing well] [AT&T] (1969) : Widely licensed multitasking operating system for workstations and minicomputers. Originally developed at Bell Laboratories, and now jointly developed by AT&T and Sun Microsystems, Inc. Distribution of the source code has brought about many varieties of implementation and extensions.

update rate : The rate at which a new image is computed and displayed. Between updates, the same image may be displayed a number of times, at the *refresh rate*.

UQUM \ *uck-um* \ [from PHIGS] : *U*se *Q*uick *U*pdate *M*ethods; command mechanism that allows the use of an erase and repaint method for making a change in a graphics image. Repaint methods are often imperfect, leaving small errors on the screen. When the errors accumulate to a level of distraction, the user commands regeneration of the entire image.

user application : Program that is running as part of a user's process on the local machine or a remote machine.

user process : Software including the user application and the window interface and, possibly, copied portions of graphics system libraries.

uucp \ *U-U-C-P* \ : *UNIX* to *UNIX CoPy*; the collection of programs that implements the mail and news functions associated with UNIX.

V

Valid Logic, Inc. : San Jose, CA, company producing systems for electronic circuit design.

valuator device [originally GKS terminology] : A computer input device that provides absolute numbers as inputs, such as from dials and knobs, rather than relative data, such as from a mouse or track ball.

value *n.* : The property of a color that is proportional to the illumination level or source brightness.

value-added reseller : —See VAR.

vaporware [*slang*] *n.* : A promised product that has not become available on schedule.

VAR *V-A-R* or, occasionally, *var*\\ : *V*alue-*A*dded *R*eseller; a manufacturer who buys computer equipment, adds software or peripherals, and sells the resulting integrated system to end users.

VAX™ *vacks*\\ [trademark, DEC] *adj.* : Having a computer architecture proprietary to Digital Equipment Corp., embodied in a successful family of minicomputer and workstation products. Also, *n.* : a computer built using the VAX architecture.

VCR : *V*ideo *C*assette *R*ecorder; any device recording video signals on cassette (as opposed to reel-to-reel) tape.

VDM : *V*irtual *D*evice *M*etafile; —See CGI [2].

VDU : *V*isual *D*isplay *U*nit; an alphanumeric terminal or other interactive device having a CRT display.

vector *n.* 1 : In graphics, a line segment described by two vertices, generally without an implied order. 2 : In mathematics, a directed line segment.

vector dither : A dithering method in which the dither matrix is oriented along the length of a line, rather than being fixed in screen space.

vectorgraphic displays : A class of displays having individually addressable pixels, usually without shades of gray (i.e., just on and off), which are written at less than video rates. This includes certain types of liquid crystal displays and other types of flat panel displays, as well as some large sign-board types of displays.

vector quantization : A means of compressing an image that involves dividing the image into small blocks of pixels, sorting the blocks into groups that are similar, and encoding the image as a sequence of addresses into a relatively small table of blocks typifying each of the sorted groups. The method works especially well with graphics-originated imagery. The computer time required for compression is relatively long, but reconstruction is rapid. The name of the method is derived from conceptualizing each block's image data as representing the coordinates of a vector in multidimensional space, so that grouping similar blocks corresponds to finding vectors that are close together.

verification suite : A test suite developed using formal and semiformal methods of program verification, as opposed to manual test development. The objective is to provide input data and commands to a graphics system together with analysis of the output so as to ensure that the system is conforming to specifications. For example, the verification suite is typically run after bug fixes to ensure that secondary errors were not induced by the fixes.

Verilog : A tool for system-level simulation using both C language and gate-level models.

verso *n.* : In typesetting, the left-hand page, particularly with respect to page format as it differs from right-hand pages. —Compare RECTO.

vertex *n.* : One of the points determining the edges of a polygon, polyhedra, or other graphics object.

vertex normal : A normalized vector specified at each polygon vertex for the purpose of subsequent illumination calculations. The vertex normal is sometimes computed as the average of the surface normals of the surrounding polygons; later interpolation of these normals when the polygons are processed independently minimizes the appearance of faceting.

Vertex Normal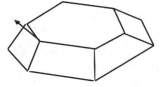

vertical resolution 1 : In raster graphics, the number of scanlines visible in the vertical dimension of a display. 2 : In video systems, the number of horizontal lines that can be reproduced by a camera and monitor, typically fewer than the number of scanlines.

vertical retrace 1 : In a CRT display system, the blanked return of the electron beam from the bottom of the display to the top. 2 : The vertical retrace interval : the time taken to accomplish vertical retrace.

Very Large Scale Integration : —See VLSI.

VEX *vecks*\ : *V*ideo *E*xtension for *X*-windows; proposed specification for integrating video input and output into the X-windows environment, including control of signal routing and blending with graphics imagery.

VGA™ *V-G-A*\ [IBM] : *V*ideo *G*raphics *A*rray; standard interface and frame buffer specification for 480 x 640 and 800 x 600 pixel color for MS-DOS personal computers. **Super VGA** is a set of extensions to 1024 x 768 and higher resolutions. By one count, there are 17 combinations of screen resolution, bits-per-pixel, and interlacing within the scope of VGA.

VGEN *V-gen*\ : A software product used to generate functional test vectors for circuits.

VHDL *V-H-D-L*\ : *V*ery *H*igh-Level *D*efinition *L*anguage; an IEEE-standardized language for the specification of electronic circuits and systems at a high level, i.e., at the register level and above.

VHS™ *V-H-S*\ [Japan Victor Corp.] : *V*ideo *H*ome *S*ystem; a widely licensed format for the recording of television video on half-inch-tape cassettes. A variation called *Super* VHS (*S-VHS*) provides separate I/O cabling and recording channels for the luminance and chrominance components of the video signal.

VHSIC *vissick*\ : *V*ery *H*igh-*S*peed *I*ntegrated *C*ircuit Program; a 1980s project sponsored by the U.S. government to encourage the availability of advanced high-speed integrated circuit technology suitable for military applications.

via *n.* : An electrical connection through insulating layers, as through layers of a printed circuit board or through oxide on an integrated circuit.

via point *n.* : An intermediate location through which a manipulator must pass in reaching its ultimate position.

vibrotactile *adj.* : Related to devices that communicate by vibrating to stimulate the sense of touch, such as a controller that vibrates to signal an event having occurred; a classic example is a stick shaker used in aircraft to warn pilots of the onset of dangerous stall conditions. There are also fingertip-sized touch displays in which the tactors vibrate.

video *n.* 1 : A sequence of electronic images for continuous viewing, as the visual portion of television. 2 : The signals that encode or transfer such an image sequence.

videoconference *n.* : Teleconference with video images of the participants communicated as well as voice. —See also, TELE-CONFERENCE.

Video Graphics Array : —See VGA.

video modes : On graphics adapters for IBM-compatible personal computers, alternate selections for the screen resolution and number of colors available for display.

video random access memory : —See VRAM.

videotex *n.* : A display of text and simple, typically colorful, graphics locally rendered from a relatively low-bandwidth stream of encoded drawing commands. The low bandwidth permits the commands to be sent over phone lines or encoded as part of a broadcast television signal. Also, *adj.* : videotex-related.

viewing coordinates : Coordinate system including all of the coordinate transformations in a graphics pipeline except perspective projection.

viewpoint *n.* : The coordinates of the point used for the computation of a particular graphics image; sometimes used loosely to include the direction and angles of view needed to define the transformations and clipping planes for the image : VIEWING LOCATION : EYEPOINT : VIRTUAL CAMERA POINT.

viewport *n.* : A defined portion of a display screen for rendering graphics, especially in the context of *GKS*.

virtual camera : The viewpoint, viewing direction, and angles of view needed to define the transformation and clipping planes to render a graphics image.

virtual device [in GKS] : A standard representation of a graphics input or output device having, for example, a predefined coordinate space. Software provides the required interface, including transformation, from the physical device to the virtual device.

virtual device coordinate space : In graphics processing, an intermediate coordinate system used for three-dimensional operations after the viewing transformations. Typically, the origin is at the viewpoint, the z-axis is in the direction of view, and the x- and y-axes are parallel to the horizontal and vertical clipping planes, respectively.

Virtual Device Metafile : —See CGI [2].

virtual environment [believed to have been coined at NASA Ames Research Center, in preference to the oxymoronic "virtual reality"] *n.*: VIRTUAL REALITY, ARTIFICIAL REALITY.

virtual memory : Implementation of a hierarchy of memory, typically including cache, main memory, and hard disk storage, to hide the physical dependencies so that an applications programmer may treat a large address space as if all storage were in main memory.

virtual reality [coined by Jaron Lanier, c. 1987] *n.* 1. : An electronic simulation in which perspective images are generated in real time from a stored database corresponding to the position and orientation of the head of a user, who observes the images on a head mounted display. 2. : An electronic simulation in which images are generated in real time or near real time from a stored database and displayed in such a way as to facilitate real-time interaction with the database, such as a vehicle simulation with imagery presented for viewing out the windows of the vehicle. 3. : Most generally, any electronic simulation or display that suggests the sense of involvement or interaction associated with virtual reality as practiced using head mounted displays. —See also IMMERSIVE VIRTUAL REALITY, ARTIFICIAL REALITY, VIRTUAL ENVIRONMENT.

visual acuity : The maximum resolving power of the human eye, about one milliradian.

visual computing : Programmed computational techniques for the creation and manipulation of digital images and graphics.

visual display unit : —See VDU.

visualization *n.* : The process of representing data as a visual image. The data may have been originally conceived as representing a world with recognizable features, such as a model of a room interior that is visualized as a recognizable room, perhaps as a design aid prior to constructing the room. Abstract data may also be visualized, by converting the data into a visual analog; the classic example is a simple graph, but more exotic three-dimensional representations of data are now typically implied. —See also SCIENTIFIC VISUALIZATION, DATA VISUALIZATION.

vivid *adj.* : Having high color saturation : pure or nearly pure in color.

VLSI *V-L-S-I*\ : *Very Large Scale Integration*; the class of integrated circuit devices having a complexity of roughly 2000 to 200,000 gates, or the equivalent. [Some sources extend the upper boundary to one million gates or more.]

VMEbus *V-M-E-bus*\ : Asynchronous processor and I/O bus standard (IEEE P1014), used extensively in workstations for I/O.

VMS™ *V-M-S*\ : Proprietary operating system for DEC VAX computers.

volume rendering : Producing an image from a three-dimensional set of data, usually scientific or engineering data : **volume visualization.**

voxel *n.* : [apparently from *volume* pi*xel*] One of an array of equal-sized cubes conceptually subdividing a three-dimensional space.

VPL Research : a Silicon Valley company, now defunct, that pioneered in virtual reality products.

VRAM *V-ram*\\ : *V*ideo *R*andom *A*ccess *M*emory; a type of dynamic memory IC having a shift register for serial output well-suited to the display video application in a graphics system.

VST \\from Truevision's VISTA frame buffer products\\ : File format for color imagery, an extension of the TGA format.

W

WAC window *wack window*\\ : Wide *Area* Collimating *window;* an optical assembly typically used in flight simulation in which a CRT is viewed via a curved mirror so as to enlarge the image and collimate it.

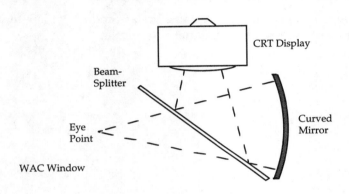

waldo [from a book character] *n.* : A computer input device worn on the head for measuring elements of facial expression as a means of controlling the corresponding elements of the expressions of computer-generated animated characters.

walking menu : —See MENU.

WAN : Wide *Area* Network; a computer network interconnecting users over a large geographical area, generally serving hundreds to thousands of users.

wand *n.* : A sticklike pointing device tracked to provide computer inputs for a virtual reality system.

Warnock's algorithm [originated by John Warnock, 1969] : A method of solving the hidden-surface problem by recursively subdividing the image area until, in each region, a single polygon is found to be occluding all the other polygons in that region, or other simple occlusion conditions are met.

warping *n.* : Two-dimensional mapping of an input image to yield an output image.

waterfall *n.* : —*See* FUZZY RUG.

150

Wavefront Technologies : Santa Barbara, CA, company producing software for high-quality rendering; their customer base has been mainly television, advertising, and entertainment, but engineering and scientific visualization applications are now growing.

Webber's law : That the just-detectable change in luminance is a constant percentage of the luminance over a wide range of luminance values. This is equivalent to a logarithmic model for the perception of luminance, a reasonably good approximation, but now a cube-root model is preferred. —See also, CIELUV.

weight *n.* : In typography, the thickness of stroke and consequent appearance of lightness or darkness characterizing a typefont, boldface being a heavier weight than normal type, for example.

Weiler-Atherton algorithm [originated by K. Weiler and P. Atherton, 1977] : An area-subdivision algorithm for hidden surface removal in which the image area is subdivided along polygon boundaries until in each region of subdivision a condition of simple occlusion is met.

weld *v.t.* : To convert nearby vertices to a common set of coordinate values in order to cure cracking.

white level *n.* : In a display system, the upper limit for signals corresponding to white inputs.

white space : In publishing, the blank space left on a page, especially as it relates to the aesthetics of the page appearance.

WID *wid*, rhymes with *hid*\\ : Window Identifier, a value stored with each pixel used to identify the associated window, color mode, or other attribute of the pixel.

wide area collimating window : —See WAC WINDOW.

wide area network : —See WAN.

widow *n.* : In publishing, the last line of text of a paragraph, especially if it has one word and falls at the end of a column or page. —Compare ORPHAN.

WID RAM : Window Identifier Random Access Memory; the table of color modes used to decode the WID values on output.

Winchester [from the *Winchester* firearms company; one story has it that "thirty-thirty" was common terminology for the Winchester 30-30 rifle and for the development disk drive that had two 30-megabyte units.] *adj.* : Of a hard disk drive, produced as a sealed unit to keep out contamination, now the common practice.

winding rule : A means for determining if a point is inside or outside of a generalized polygon by summing the angles with respect to the point.

window *n.* : A collection of one or more rasters plus additional properties, and usually having borders and other graphics elements established by the conventions of the window system. Users typically associate a window with the screen output of a task in a multitasking environment. —See also RASTER.

window ID planes : Memory space associated with each pixel of a display dedicated to identifying which window is associated with that pixel (the *WID)* and used to clip new graphics imagery to the appropriate window.

window interface : A package of software that runs as part of the user process and includes functions that are not available directly from the window server (e.g., scroll bars, buttons, pop-up menus); also called an *application programmer's interface* (API).

window server : Portion of a window system that controls access to the display devices by allocating rasters and controls access to the associated input devices; examples are X11 /NeWS and X11 /PEX.

window system : A software system for sharing graphics input and output devices, including the association of client applications with distinct regions on a display.

wireframe : An image in which only the edges of polygonal surfaces are displayed, drawn as vectors. —Compare HOLLOW FILL.

wobulator *n.* : A device for widening the raster line on a CRT display by injecting a deflection signal at a frequency higher than the line rate. Used, for example, in adapting a conventional color shadowmask CRT (designed for horizontal scan) to vertical scan when the beam would not otherwise cover the phosphor triad.

word processing [*alt.* wordprocessing] : Use of a computer system for the entry and manipulation of text. Generally distinct from desktop publishing in that word processing is more concerned with the content of document text while desktop publishing uses text as input to processes concerned with the appearance of the text, including font selection, page layout, and integration with figures. The distinction is becoming blurred as more software integrates both sets of features.

word wrapping : WRAPAROUND [1].

workcell *n.* : A collection of robotic manipulators and other equipment assembled in proximity to perform a set of tasks.

workspace *n.* : The range of positions reached by a robotic manipulator.

workstation *n.* : A high-performance computer closely coupled to a high-resolution graphics display. One older definition is "a computer designed for a single user having at least 1 MB of storage, executing at least 1.0 MIPS, and having a bit-mapped display with at least one million pixels." Some maintain there is a qualitative distinction in that workstations are designed primarily for performance and secondarily for ease of use, as opposed to personal computers where the priorities are reversed. The difference between a personal computer and a workstation is not perfectly well defined, but workstations occupy the high end of personal computing devices.

world coordinates : The coordinate system of the application's database.

WORM : *Write-Once Read-Many*; applied to laser disk storage devices that cannot be erased.

WPM : A file extension designating an object-oriented file format compatible with the *Microsoft Windows* interface.

wraparound *n*. 1 : A common feature in word processors allowing text to be entered without carriage returns, with the program providing automatic continuation to the next line of the display or printed document. 2 : The unintended continuation of a drawn display element extending beyond a screen edge to the opposite edge of the screen, a condition prevented by *scissoring*.

wrapper *n*. : A layer of software built upon a preestablished package to convert the format of the calls, the data stores, and the like to a new format or interface standard.

wrapping *n*. : WRAPAROUND.

WTDS : *Worldwide Phosphor Type Designation System*; a system for designating the phosphors used in CRTs by one or two letters. Established in 1982, replacing an older system in which phosphors were designated by *P* plus a number.

WYSIWYG *wizzy wig*\ *n*. : What You See Is What You Get; property of a graphics software application, usually for desktop publishing, in which the output on the computer display screen is similar to that produced for the printed page. The printed output usually has higher resolution than the screen, but corresponds to the display in terms of fonts and layout. Applications that are not WYSIWYG often show a control sequence on the screen which is replaced with the commanded action on the paper output; for example, a command .bo on the screen might disappear on output, having caused the following line to be printed in boldface.

X

X *n.* 1 : The X Window System. 2 : The WTDS designation of the phosphors used in color television, previously called P22G, P22R, and P22B.

X.11 \X *eleven*\ [*alt.* X11] : The 11th version of the *X Window System.*

X.25 \X *dot twenty-five*\ : A CCITT standard for computer communication on public data networks using packet switching techniques.

X3H3 : The American National Standards Committee concerned with graphics.

x-axis : The horizontal axis in two-dimensional graphics, conventionally positive to the right.

XDR : EXternal *D*ata *R*epresentation; a mechanism for sharing data among different computers over a network. —See also, ONC.

XENIX™ : [Microsoft] A clone of the UNIX operating system originated by Microsoft for personal computers.

xerography *n.* : Printing and copying technology in which an image is formed by an electrostatic charge on a drum, and the charge is subsequently used to attract a toner that is transferred to paper where the toner is fused by heat. Also, *adj.* : **xerographic.**

Xerox Network System : —See XNS.

XGL™ : *S*un *G*raphics *L*anguage; a low-level graphics language originated by Sun Microsystems.

x height : The height of the lowercase letters in a font exclusive of ascenders and descenders, as typified by the letter "x." Larger x height is generally associated with improved readability of a font.

Xilinx \ZI-*links*\ : San Jose, CA, manufacturer of logic cell array integrated circuits, conceptually much like a software-configurable gate array.

XNS \X-N-S\ : *X*erox *N*etwork *S*ystem; an architecture for interprocess communication across a network.

XOR \X-*or*\ *n.* 1 : EXclusive *OR*; a logic function in which the output is true if one, and only one, of two inputs are true. 2 : The result of applying the XOR function <C is the XOR of signals A and B>. Also, *v.*: To perform the XOR function. XORs, XORed, XORing.

XT : Originally, an IBM PC/XT personal computer using an Intel 8088 processor and distinguished from the plain IBM PC by having a hard disk. Now used for any IBM-compatible 8088-based personal computer.

X terminal : A device for receiving input and displaying text and graphics output in accordance with the standards of the X Window System, but lacking general-purpose computer capabilities.

XView™ [Sun Microsystems] : Toolkit for implementing OPEN LOOK.

X Window System [The developers prefer that the name not be shortened to "X Windows", the name "X" was derived as the successor to a window system named "W," which in turn was associated with a Stanford University operating system named *"V"*™][MIT] : A window system originated at MIT for networked UNIX applications, now widely adopted as an industry standard.

xyY space : A CIE-based coordinate space for specifying color and intensity. The (x,y) coordinates are the chromaticity components, and Y is the luminance. Since in the CIE system the three color components (x,y,z) add to one, no information is lost by dropping z. The *x, y* and *z* are obtained by normalizing X,Y, and Z by dividing each component, respectively, by (X+Y+Z).

XYZ space : The CIE coordinate space for specifying colors; the tristimulus coordinate space.

Y

Y *n.* : The luminance component of an encoded-color video signal or of a color coordinate space. —See YIQ SPACE.

yaw *n.* : The angular displacement of a vehicle or device about the vertical axis, in the plane of the longitudinal and lateral axes.

y-axis : The vertical axis in two-dimensional graphics. Usually the positive direction is upwards for applications programs, but screen coordinates for a raster display are often defined with y positive downwards on the screen.

YIQ space [*Y* traditional for luminance, *I* for the in-phase signal, and *Q* for the quadrature signal] : The color space of NTSC television, in which the brightness (Y), orange-cyan (I), and green-magenta (Q) components are assigned successively lower bandwidths. The encoding is also used for digital compression or storage by assigning successively fewer bits to the components. The economies are achieved by taking advantage of the human eye's respectively decreasing sensitivity to changes in these parameters.

YMCK [less common *alt.* to CMYK] : Yellow, Magenta, Cyan, Key; —See CMYK.

yon *n.* 1. : A clipping plane perpendicular to the line-of-sight used to exclude distant objects; the back clipping plane. 2. : The distance along the line-of-sight from the viewpoint to the back clipping plane.

Yourdon method : A method of systems analysis and design involving structure charts and data flow diagrams; sometimes called the *Yourdon-DeMarco method.*

Z

z *n.* : In the calculation of a graphics image, the perpendicular distance from a point on an object to the plane through the viewpoint that is parallel to the image plane; preferred to the straightforward distance to the point because it is easier to compute.

z-axis 1 : In three-dimensional graphics, the depth axis. 2 : In calligraphic displays and some [older] video contexts, the brightness component of a drawn image. 3 : In pressure-sensitive data tablets, the pressure component of a drawn input.

Zapf dingbats [originated by typefont designer Hermann Zapf] [ITC Zapf Dingbats is a trademark of International Type Corp.] : A particular set of symbols, including various squares, dots, arrows, and the like, widely used in typography.

z-buffer : Array of stored z values associated with the pixels in an image and used to perform occlusion.

zel [uncommon] *n.* : A depth value, as stored in a z-buffer.

zit-blit [uncommon] *n.* : A pixel area copy (bitblt) bringing along z-buffer values as well, and performing a z-compare during the copy.

zoom *v.i.* : To change the scale of a view of a two-dimensional database, or to change the field-of-view of a view of a three-dimensional database. For **hardware zoom** the image is precomputed and a portion selected is enlarged by repeating pixels or reduced by omitting pixels.

zoom pyramid : A sequence of digital images starting with a high-resolution image in which each successive image is computed as a lower-resolution version of the previous. Typically, a power of two separates resolutions so that four pixels reduce to one in each successive stage. Zoom pyramids are used in image processing and for texture mapping in graphics, wherein the desired resolution of an image or pattern is derived by linear interpolation between the levels of the pyramid. Note that storing the whole pyramid requires only one-third more storage than the highest resolution alone. —See also, MIP MAP.

Word List

The word list below is intended as an aid in spell-checking. It includes all of the general terminology in the body of this dictionary, plus additional variants of the terms such as plurals and possessives. The variants are included mainly for compatibility with spell-checking software that needs to be told the variants explicitly. There are also a number of terms in this list not in the body of the dictionary, mainly common technical jargon that nonetheless failed to be recognized by one or more spell-checking programs. For inclusion in this list, each word had to have been omitted from the lists of at least one of three spell-checking programs tried by the author.

A

ABI
accuracies
ACM
ACM's
acronymed
adaptively
Addison
addressability
AFD
affine
airbrushing
AIX
aliased
aliasing
alphanumeric
alphanumerics
Altera
Altera's
AMD
AMD's
Amdek
Amdek's
amps
anaglyph
ANDed

ANDing
ANDs
anisotropic
annualized
ANSI
antialias
antialiased
antialiases
antialiasing
API
Apollo
Apollo's
apostilb
architected
architecting
ARPANET
ARPANET's
arsenide
ascender
ascenders
ASIC
ASICs
asynchronous
asynchronously
ATG
Atherton

atomically
AutoCAD
AutoCAD's
autoconfiguration
autocorrelation
autodimension
autodimensioned
autodimensioning
autodimensions
Autofact
AVL
awk

B

backfacing
backplane
backplanes
backslash
backslashes
bandwidth
bandwidths
barfogenic zone
Barsky
baseline
baselines

baud
Baudot
BCPL
beamsplitter
beamsplitters
benchmark
benchmarked
benchmarking
benchmarks
Berkeley
Bezier
BiCMOS
bicubic
bilinear
biocular
BioDesign
BioSym
bitblt
bit map
blacker
blendmap
Blinn
blit
blits
blitted
blondel
blondels
BOM
Boolean
Borland
Borland's
Borrill
bpi
breezeway
Bresenham
Bresenham's
Brigham
brightness
brightnesses
Brooktree
Brooktree's
BSP

BW
BYU

C

cacheable
CACM
CADCAM
CADD
CADDS
CADDs
Cadroid
CAE
CAI
calligraphically
Calma
Cartesian
Catmull
CAV
CCD
CCITT
CD
cel
CG
CGA
CGI
CGM
chroma
chromakey
chromakeyed
chromakeying
chromakeys
chromas
chrominance
CIELUV
CIM
CISC
clipbox
CLV
CMAP
CMOS
CMY
CMYK

codec
codecs
Cohen
collimate
collimated
collimates
collimating
collimation
collimator
collimators
colorimetry
colorize
colorized
colorizes
colorizing
COM
combinational
COMDEX
Compaq
comparitor
comparitors
composited
composites
compositing
CompuServe
CompuServe's
computationally
ComputerVision
ComputerVision's
configurable
configure
connectivity
Conrac
Conrac's
convolve
convolver
convolvers
convolvers
convolves
convolving
Convolvotron
Cooley

coplanar
coplanarity
coprocessor
coprocessors
couleur
CPUs
Cray
Cray's
Crays
crosshair
CRT
CRTs
CrystalEyes
CSG
CTF
cubics
Cupertino
curvilinear
CV
CY
cyan
cyber-
cyberia
cybernaut
cyberpunk
cybersex
cyberspace
cyclically

D
DAC
DACs
daemon
Dainippon
DataGlove
dataless
dataspace
DataSuit
DCT
DDA
DDES
deallocate
deallocated
deallocates
deallocating

deassert
deasserted
deasserting
deasserts
debounce
debugger
debuggers
declutter
decluttered
decluttering
declutters
DECnet
decoder
decremented
degauss
degaussing
DeMarco
denormalize
denormalized
denormalizes
denormalizing
descender
descenders
deskside
desktop
DFD
DGIS
diagrammatically
DIF
differencing
differentiable
digitally
digitization
digitizer
digitizers
dimensionality
dimmest
dingbat
dingbats
discretes
diskette
diskettes
diskfull
diskless
displayable
DMA

DOA
DORE
downloadable
downloaded
downloading
downloads
DP
DPCM
DPE
dpi
DRC
DSEE
DSP
DTP
Duff
DVI
DVMA
Dvorak
DVST

E
EBCDIC
ECAD
ECAE
ECC
ECD
ECL
ECO
ECP
EDIF
editable
EEPROM
EEPROMs
EGA
EGAs
EIA
EIA's
Eikonix
EISA
electromechanical
electronique
electrophotographic
emittance
emitter
emitters

en
end-effector
enqueue
enqueued
enqueueing
enqueues
ens
EPLD
EPROM
EPROMs
Epson
ESD
ethernet
Eurocard
Evans
expandability
exponentials
extensible
eyepoint
eyepoints

F
fab
faceplate
faceted
faceting
FAQ
FARs
fax
FCC
FCS
FDDI
FEA
featurism
FEM
Feshner's
FFT
fiberoptic
FIFO
FIFOs
firmware
flatbed

FLIR
Foley
footcandle
footcandles
footlambert
footlamberts
Fourier
FOV
fovea
foveal
FPA
fractal
fractals
fractionally
fractus
fresnel
frisket
FRU
FST
FTG
Futurebus
FY

G
GaAs
GALs
Gantt
genlock
genlocked
genlocking
geospecific
GIF
gigabyte
gigaflop
GIS
GKS
Glassner
Gouraud
GPCI
graftal
graphical
grayscale

greek
greeking
GSS
GUI
Gupta
GVG
GVS

H
halation
halftoning
haloed
haptic
hard copy
HDTV
Helvetica
hemi
Hermite
Hershey
Hewlett
hexadecimal
hexcone
HIL
hiragana
Hodgman
hotspot
HPGL
HR
HSL
HSV
Hubbard
HUD
Huffman
HW
hyperboloids
HyperCard
hypermedia
hypertext
Hz

I
IBM

IBM's
IC
iconify
ICS
ID's
IEEE
IELAB
IGES
ilities
illuminance
illuminant
illuminants
IMSI
IMSI's
inbetween
inbetweening
inbetweens
Inc
incrementally
instancing
instantiated
instantiation
instrumented
Intel
Intel's
interactively
interactivity
interchangeability
interchangeably
Intercon
interconnection
interconnections
interframe
interglyph
Interleaf
Interleaf's
Internationale
internet
internetwork
internetworking
interocular
  distance
interpenetrate
interpenetrates
interpenetration
interprocess

interprocessor
intervisibility
interworking
ip
IrisGL
IRIX
ISBN
ISDN
ISO
isosurface
ISV
iteratively
IU

J

jaggles
jitter
jittering
joystick
joysticks
JPEG
JTAG

K

Kajiya
kana
kanji
katakana
Kaufmann
kermit
kernel
kernels
Kernighan
kerning
keyframe
Knuth
KV
Kyocera

L

L'Eclairage
lacunar
lacunarity
Lambert's
LAN
leadless

LEDs
Leffler
LeMer
Lempel
letterform
letterforms
linearization
LOD
logarithmically
Lowell
lowercase
LSI
LSSD
Lucasfilm
LUT
LUTs
Luv
lux
LW
LZW

M

Mac
MacDraw
Machover
Macintosh
MacPaint
macroassembler
macroparallelism
Mandelbrot
manipulandum
maskable
matrixed
Mb
MBytes
MCAD
MCAE
McDonnell
McGraw
MDE
mega
megaflops
memoire
metaball
Metafile
metamer

metameric
metastable
metastablization
MFLOPS
MHEG
MHz
Mhz
microcode
microcoded
microfacet
microfacets
MicroSoft
Microsystems
microVAX
millilambert
milliradian
MIMD
minification
minified
minify
MIPS
MIPs
MIS
MIT
MMU
modem
modems
modulus
mono
monohedral
motherboard
Motorola
MP
MPEG
MPSD
MR
msec
msp
MTBF
MTF
MTS
MTV

multi
multibus
Multics
multimodal
multipass
multiplexor
multiprocessing
multiprocessor
multiprocessors
multitasking
Munsell
mux
muxed

N

NAND
NANDed
NANDing
NANDs
nanoseconds
NAPLPS
NCGA
NDK
netlist
Newell
Newman
NeWS
NeXT
NFS
nitere
noncondensing
nonintersecting
nonlacunar
nonlinear
nonlinearly
nonoperating
nonuniform
NORed
NORing
NORs
Nostrand
Noyes

NPG
NPI
ns
nsec
nsecs
NTSC
Nubus
NURB
nybble

O

OA
obsolesced
Occam
OCR
octant
octree
OEM
OEMs
Omura
ONC
opcode
ops
optimizer
Optronix
ORed
ORing
ORs
OS
OSF
OSI
overlayed
oversampled
oversampling
ownship

P

Packard
PALs
paraboloids
parallelograms
parameterized

parametric
PARC
patentable
Patran
PCB
PCL
PCX
pel
penetron
perspectively
PEX
PGA
phaselock
PHIGS
Phong
phot
photomapped
photomapping
photometric
photopic
photoplotter
PIC
PICT
pictographic
piecewise
pinout
pinouts
pipelined
Pitteway
pixel
pixel's
pixellization
pixels
pixmap
planar
PLCC
PNR
Polhemus
polyhedra
polyhedron
polyline
polylines
polymarker
polymarkers
ported
porting

POSIX
posterization
posterize
postprocessing
PostScript
PowerGlove
Pratt
precomputed
predefined
preemptive
prefekhing
prefetch
preprocessed
preprocessing
preselected
Primavera
Primavision
Princeton
prioritization
prioritized
proactive
prototile
prototyped
prototyping
PS
pseudoblanking
pseudocolor
pseudocolored
pseudocoloring
pseudorandom
Purkinje
purplish

Q
QDL
QE
quadric
quadtree
quantization
quantized
quantizer
quartic
qwerty

R
radially

radiosity
RAMDAC
RAMDACs
RAMdisk
raster
rasterization
rasterize
rasterizes
rasterizing
rasterop
rasters
RBG
readback
recirculate
recirculates
reconfigure
reconfigured
reconfiguring
recursive
recursively
redesign
redesigned
redesigning
redraw
redrawing
redrawn
reentrant
reformating
Reinhold
RenderMan
renormalization
repaint
repainted
repainting
repaints
repositioned
repositioning
reprogram
reprogrammed
rerendered
rescanned
reseller
reserialize
resize
resizing
retroreflectivity

reused
revolute joint
rewinding
RFI
RFIs
RFP
RFPs
RFQ
RFQs
RFr
RGB
RISC
RJ
RLL
robotic
Rogers
ROI
ROM
Roncarelli
ROP
ROPs
Roth
router
RPC
RS
RTP
runarounds

S

SABRE
sans-serif
SCA
scalable
scaleless
scalings
scanline
scanlines
Schumacher
SCI
scissoring
SCO
scotopic
SCS
SCSI
SDRC
SECAM

Seiko
selectability
selectable
sequencer
serially
server's
SGI
SGI's
shader
shadowmask
shippable
siccade
SIE
SIGGRAPH
sketchpad
SMD
SMT
Snell's
SNR
socketing
soft copy
SOIC
SOJ
Sony
Sony's
SpaceBall
SPARC
SPEC
specifier
spectrophotometer
specular
splat
splats
spline
splines
splitter
Spox
Sproull
Sproull's
SSI
staircasing
stairstepped
stairstepping
standalone
Stanford
statefull

statusing
Stereographics
stilb
stochastic
stroker
styli
subassemblies
subindenture
subindentured
subpixel
subpixels
subscripted
subtasks
subtier
succolar
succolarity
SunGL
Sunnyvale
SunTrak
superblack
superblock
superblue
supercase
supercomputer
supercomputing
superconic
superconics
superellipsoid
superellipsoids
supergreen
supermini
superposed
superquadric
superquadrics
superred
supersample
supersampled
supersampling
superscalar
superscripted
supershift
superuser
superwhite
supportability
supportable
Sutherland

Sutherland's
SW
swash
synch
synchronism
systeme

T
TA
TAAC
tactor
Tannas
TBD
TCP
Tektronix
telecon
teleconferencing
teledildonics
teleoperation
telerobotics
teletex
Teradyne
teraflop
tesselation
tesselations
testability
testable
texel
texels
texturing
Thompson
thresholding
thumbwheel
thumbwheels
TI
TI's
TIF
TIFF
TIGA
TM
TMS
tomography
toners
toolkit
topological
topologically

topologies
topology
tori
toroidal
torus
trackball
tracker
tradeoffs
transitioning
traversal
triboluminescence
trinitron
tristate
tristimulus
TSR
Tsui
TTL
Tukey
TV
TVF
tween
tweened
tweening
tweens
typefont
typeset
typesetting

U
UCLA
UL
ULSI
unaccelerated
unaligned
unbundled
unbundling
uncacheable
underflow
underflows
Underwood
undithered
UNIBUS
uninterruptable
UniSys
UNIX
unmap

unmapped
unmapping
unoccluded
unpolarized
unselected
Upstill
UQUM
uucp

V
vaporware
VAR
VARs
VAX
VAXes
VCR
VCRs
VDC
VDE
VDM
VDT
VDTs
VDU
VDUs
vectorgraphic
vectorization
Verilog
Verlag
VGA
VGEN
VHDL
VHS
VHSIC
vias
vibrotactile
videoconference
videotex
viewgraph
viewgraphs
viewport
VLSI
VME
VMEbus
VMS
voxel
voxels

VP
VRAM

W
WAC
waldo
walkthrough
walkthroughs
wand
Warnock
Warnock's
Watkinson
waveform
waveforms
Wavefront
Webber's
Weiler
Welch
Wesley
Whitted
WID
WIDs
Wiley

Winchester
wireframe
wireframes
wobulator
WordPerfect
wordprocessed
wordprocessing
WordStar
workaround
workarounds
workcell
workstation
workstations
wpm
WTDS
Wyse
WYSIWYG

X
XDR
XENIX
XGL
Xilinx

XLIB
XNS
XOR
XORed
XORing
XORs
XT
XView
xyY
xyz

Y
YIQ
YMCK
Yourdon

Z
Zapf
zel
zit
Ziv

Bibliography

Bartels, Richard H., et al. (1987). *An Introduction to Splines for Use in Computer Graphics ~ Geometric Modeling.* Los Altos, Calif.: Morgan Kaufmann Publishers, Inc.

Borrill, Paul (July 1989). "High-speed 32-bit buses for forward-looking computers," *IEEE Spectrum,* vol. 26, no. 7, p. 34.

Conrac Corp. (1985). *Raster Graphics Handbook,* second ed. New York: Van Nostrand Reinhold Co.

Foley, James D., Andries van Dam, et al. (1990). *Computer Graphics Principles and Practice,* second ed., Reading, Mass. : Addison-Wesley Publishing Co.

Glassner, Andrew S. (Ed.) (1989). *An Introduction to Ray Tracing.* London: Academic Press.

Hamit, Francis (1993). *Virtual Reality and the Exploration of Cyberspace,* Carmel, Calif. : SAMS Publishing.

Hearn, Donald, and M. Pauline Baker (1986). *Computer Graphics.* Englewood Cliffs, N.J. : Prentice-Hall, Inc.

Hubbard, Stuart W. (1983). *The Computer Graphics Glossary.* Phoenix, Ariz. : Oryx Press.

James, Glenn, and R. C. James (1968). *Mathematics Dictionary.* Princeton, N.J. : D. Van Nostrand Co.

Kalawsky, Ray (1993). *The Science of Virtual Reality and Virtual Environments,* Wokingham, England: Addison-Wesley Publishing Co.

Kelly, Kenneth L., and Deane B. Judd (1976). *COLOR: Universal Language and Dictionary of Names.* NBS Special Publication 440. Washington, DC: U.S. Department of Commerce, U.S. Government Printing Office.

Leffler, Samuel J., et al. (1988). *The Design and Implementation of the 4.3 UNIX Operating System.* Reading, Mass. : Addison-Wesley Publishing Co.

Machover, Carl (Ed.) (1989). *The C4 Handbook.* Blue Ridge Summit, Pa.: Tab Books.

McConnell, John (1988). *Internetworking Computer Systems.* Englewood Cliffs, N.J. : Prentice-Hall, Inc.

Newman, William, and Robert Sproull (1979) *Principles of Interactive Computer Graphics,* second ed., New York: McGraw-Hill Book Co.

Pratt, William K. (1978). *Digital Image Processing.* New York: John Wiley & Sons.

Rogers, David F. (1985). *Procedural Elements for Computer Graphics.* New York: McGraw-Hill Book Co.

Rogers, David F., and J. A. Adams (1990). *Procedural Elements for Computer Graphics,* second ed., New York : McGraw-Hill Book Co.

Roncarelli, Robi (1989). *The Computer Animation Dictionary.* New York: Springer-Verlag.

Scheifler, Rokert W., James Gettys, and Ron Newman (1988). X *Window System.* Digital Press.

Steinhart, Johnathan, et al. (1988). *Introduction to Window Management: SIGGRAPH '88 Course* #11. Atlanta, Ga. : Association for Computing Machinery.

Sun Microsystems, Inc. (1988). *System Administration for Beginners.* Mountain View, Calif.

Tannas, Lawrence E. (Ed.) (1985). *Flat Panel Displays and CRTs.* New York: Van Nostrand Reinhold Co.

Trotti, Patricia (Ed.) (1988). *The Photonics Dictionary*™, 34th ed., Pittsfield, Mass. : Laurin Publishing Co.

Upstill, Steve (1990). *The RenderMan Companion.* Reading, Mass.: Addison-Wesley Publishing Co.

Vince, John (1984). *Dictionary of Computer Graphics,* White Plains, N.Y.: Knowledge Industry Publications, Inc.